Further Glimpses of Gayton

A Northamptonshire church and community

Rita Poxon

Sue Clayton

Published by Sue Clayton
Japonica House, Flintham
Newark, Nottinghamshire NG23 5LA

ISBN 0 9533350 4 6

Designed by © *Trevor Clayton*

Printed in Great Britain by
Technical Print Services Ltd,
Brentcliffe Avenue, Carlton Road, Nottingham NG3 7AG

Contents

Acknowledgements

The church and the community have been so closely intertwined that the story of one must reflect the story of the other. Sure enough, whilst researching the history of Gayton church, stories about village life have emerged. It has been necessary to delve into the past in a different and imaginative way but it has certainly been worth it. However, the story cannot be told simply by studying only the architecture or available documentation. The further back in time, the more important it became to look into the background of what was happening in the outside world and consider the reason behind each development. A church was reliant on enthusiastic patrons, not only for funding but as one of the driving forces behind change. The patrons' motivation was not purely the spiritual needs of the parish; their private ambitions often affected what happened locally. The cure of souls, as it was called, was the responsibility of the clergy but they, too, had their own agenda, particularly at a national level. The church authorities were anxious for power and to accumulate wealth, which ultimately they did so well that they made themselves a target for a take-over by the king. This is a complicated story that incorporates the history of religion in England, the king's supremacy, the machinations of the clergy and also the way in which the rich and well-to-do locally used the church to proclaim their own importance. The end result was that people were regulated, not only by the manor, but also by the church from birth until death. And a great deal of what they did in between was determined by both.

Many people have assisted me on the trail: Sarah Bridges, Eleanor Winyard and the staff at Northamptonshire Record Office, who are always unfailingly helpful; the Church Extension Group; all the villagers of Gayton, including those who continually search their memories for forgotten details for me, especially Eric White, Joan Adams and Wendy Briglin, and those who listen such as Anna Fox; Roger Watson, curator of the Fox Talbot Museum; and Siobhán Summerfield, archivist at the Victoria and Albert Museum. I would particularly like to thank Rachel McGrath, Senior Grants Officer, Northamptonshire Community Foundation, for funding this book; and Gayton Parish Council for additional financial support. In addition, I am grateful to the National Archives; the British Library; Family Record Centre; Centre for Kentish Studies; Warwickshire County Record Office; Wiltshire and Swindon Record Office, the University of Nottingham; Ann Davidson, Northampton Volunteering Centre; Northamptonshire Local Studies Library; Terry Fry; and my friends, Sue and Trevor Clayton. As always, it is family that bear the brunt of the tribulations and my husband, Rod, gives me great encouragement and support, but could learn a lot from the patience shown by Northamptonshire Record Office staff. Not withstanding, he has provided beautiful photographs for the book. Any errors remain my own. With the recent passing of my mother, I dedicate this publication to my parents, Richard and Vera Bennett, who allowed me to grow up in a modern world. I hope that you find the discoveries I have made both entertaining and illuminating.

Rita Poxon, MA, Gayton, July 2005

Map of Northamptonshire showing Gayton

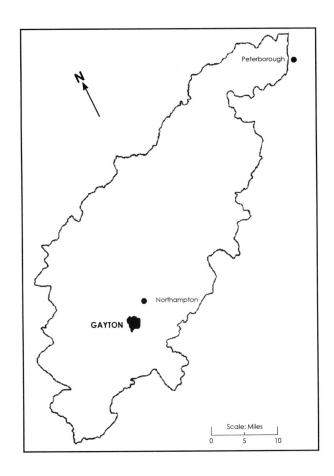

Setting the scene

Christian settlers

Gayton may not have been officially named in the Domesday Book, but we know that the early Anglo-Saxon settlers were Christian because their community of 21 villagers already had a priest living amongst them.[1] The architecture of their church supports this, too. The tiny doorway in the west wall of the church tower is typically Anglo-Saxon with its triangular headed doors and windows. During the major restoration of 1726, when the tower was raised and six bells hung, William Ball, churchwarden, carefully replicated the stonework of the west door with two huge pieces of ironstone making the apex of the triangle. William Ball was making sure that future generations would see and understand the church's Saxon importance.[2] Of course, the early Anglo-Saxon church was nothing like the church in 2005. It was probably no more than one small stone-built room, although there could have been a wooden structure attached. But, whatever its size, its site next door to the manor house sent a message to the developing village: on one hand there is the manor, and on the other the church. And both are powerful.

Norman lords bestowed land

After the Conquest in 1066, and when settled in their newly won territories, the Norman lords developed a conscience. They had, after all, been killing their fellow Christians; what would God make of that? They were anxious to earn salvation for their souls and used their immense enthusiasm for building projects to achieve this. Simon de Senlis, Earl of Northampton, built large churches such as the Holy Sepulchre in Northampton, and founded monasteries such as the Priory of St Andrew in Northampton, granting them land. Lesser men built small parish churches, and gave land or the income from some of their land to the new monasteries. In 1224, two virgates of land were made over to Northampton Hospital by Henry de Gayton; in 1836 this estate was still in hospital hands and consisted of three tenements and 37 acres of land leased by William Blake. Furthermore, Henry de

Triangular Saxon doorway
Claire, Anthony and Charlotte Ratledge

Gayton's son, Henry, gave Litevil Croft and 16 acres of Gayton land to St James Abbey in another undated grant, which was confirmed in 1298 by Hugh de Burcote. Finally, Robert of Bethune granted an annual pension of one mark from the benefice of Gayton to the abbess and nuns of Delapre, the Cluniac nunnery which had been founded by Simon de Senlis II in 1145. In this way, Robert curried favour with his lord at the same time as salving his conscience with his God. Whether Robert was also responsible for building a small church in Gayton, we cannot be sure, but sometime between 1086 and 1200 one was built.

Inside west wall of the nave. Note the old roofline and original outside edge of church through arch.

A stone church

The Normans, keen to stamp their authority on a restless population, swept away all things Anglo-Saxon and if Gayton's church had included a wooden structure, then this is when it would have been demolished. The small, stone Anglo-Saxon room was probably turned into a low tower providing the parish priest with living accommodation in the upper floor, and the nave and chancel were built on as an extension.[3] The steep line of the original roof can still be seen in 2005 as a line of broken stone protruding from the tower wall, showing that the nave was built as an integral part of the first stage of the low tower. At some time in the late nineteenth century, a south facing, round-headed window that appeared to be Norman, situated in the first stage of the tower was altered to a more pointed shape. The Victorians had a love of pointed Early English architecture as it took the eye up towards heaven and was generally thought by them to be the only true Christian form.

Setting the bounds

As early as the tenth century, the idea of payment of tithes had been introduced and the Saxon kings, Edmund, 936-946, and Edgar, 959-975, passed laws to add their weight behind the idea of everyone paying their dues to the church. The organisation of precise parish boundaries became essential, not only created by an expansion in the population, but in the proliferation of churches as well. It was important for the church authorities that everyone should be quite clear as to which church they were accountable. The necessity was made more urgent because, as the population increased, the amount of money involved also increased. This system had the additional benefit that individuals, bound by tithe-paying to a church, knew where they should attend Mass, be baptised, married and buried. The laity, with their new obligations to their parish church, could be more easily managed especially when they were seen as a continuing source of income for the clergy.

Hedge dating

Dr Max Hooper's theory of hedge dating, which he developed in the 1970s, is a far from precise science. Nevertheless, an experiment conducted in 1995 had interesting results. Taking Hooper's simplified formula that the age of a hedge equals the number of species in a 30 yard stretch, multiplied by 100, certain portions of Gayton's parish boundary were found to contain nine different species of shrubs and trees. If the hedge was 900 years old in 1995 (9 species x 100) then the hedge dated back to c.1095, thereby suggesting that the hedge was planted at the end of the eleventh century.[4] Perhaps this took place at the same time that Gayton acquired its name. To maintain the position of the parish boundary, the tradition of beating the bounds on a yearly basis developed, and in some parishes continues in 2005. However, there is a lack of evidence for this taking place in Gayton which may be explained by the early date of enclosure in 1600, when perambulating around the parish boundary would have been complicated by negotiating the multitude of new hedges and ditches.

Formal religion

The burst of activity at the beginning of the thirteenth century marks an exciting phase in the development of Gayton church. The population in England was growing, the number of churches was increasing and the existing churches were being enlarged. Both Gayton's font and the chancel piscina (stone basin) were important pieces of church furniture, both physically and liturgically, dating back to this period. A font was fundamental for baptism, which in turn was vital for the soul's salvation. It also brought every family into close contact with their parish priest and was a symbol of the personal care given to them, as well as his authority over them. This complex symbolism may explain why the font usually survived when other early trappings did not. Whatever the reason, the age of the font tells us a great deal about the age of the church. However, Gayton's font presents us with an enigma. It is unusual in its design and looks very much as though in about 1230, a

Piscina in the chancel, with nailhead moulding

3

Norman-style font was fabricated but with the current Early English influence. The pattern around the rim of the bowl would have had round arches if it had been Norman but these are more pointed and therefore lead us to consider whether it was sculpted a little later. In *The Buildings of England, Northamptonshire,* Pevsner asks whether it has been re-worked or is a form of thirteenth-century archaism.[5] Whilst the font was essential for baptism, the piscina played an equally important role in another of the sacraments, the celebration of the Mass. The piscina provided a place at the side of the altar for the priest to rinse the chalice and paten (bread holder) so the existence of a piscina indicates the presence of a nearby altar. The chancel piscina is decorated with nailhead moulding, and in contrast to the font, it bears an unashamedly thirteenth-century design. It is perhaps from this time, the early 1200s, that we can say with certainty that Gayton truly had a church and formal religion.

Our Blessed Lady, St Mary

Whether Gayton church had an earlier, different dedication is uncertain but by the fifteenth century the church was dedicated to St Mary the Virgin. Dedications to Our Lady date back to before the eighth century and reached a high level of popularity in the thirteenth century, just at the time when Gayton's church had become formalised. Not only did church dedications follow religious trends but the date of the associated feast day had implications for the congregation. St Mary had an additional bonus of several associated feast days from which to choose; the Annunciation (25 March), the Nativity (8 September) and the Assumption (15 August), although the latter was dropped from the *Book of Common Prayer* in 1549. Gayton adopted the Feast of the Nativity of the Virgin Mary with its September date, allowing the celebrations to avoid the main harvest season, always a serious consideration for villagers in a rural community.

Early English south aisle

No sooner was the church established than the next building venture, the addition of the south aisle, was embarked upon in the mid-1200s. England's population continued to grow throughout the twelfth and thirteenth century and Gayton followed the national trend with more space being needed to house the villagers at their worship. A piscina of this date was found in the south wall of the south aisle during the late Victorian restoration, further confirmation that this south aisle had been used as a chapel with its own altar. The clerk who supervised these Early English additions may well have been William de Albiniaco who was presented to the living, 21 January 1235. William, 1235-40, is the first minister to be recorded by name at Gayton, although one of his predecessors, Ralph, was named on the early, but undated grant of land to St James' Abbey.

Coffin and building works

There is little to connect the ever-growing, early church with its individual patrons except for a stone coffin lid decorated with a beautiful floriated cross, which in 2005 can be found in

Foliate cross decorating stone coffin lid

the north chapel. This must have been a memorial to someone extremely important in Gayton even though it was found upside down in the north chapel at the time of the late Victorian restoration. This may seem disrespectful to us, but it was not uncommon for memorial slabs and stones to be re-used in later building works. It does mean however, that when the north chapel was built in the fourteenth century, the family to whom the coffin was relevant had ceased to have a connection with Gayton.

Speculate to accumulate

There are three early Gayton families whose members would be candidates for both the building works and the coffin: the de Bethune, de Guisne or de Fiennes families, all of whom had an interest in the Gayton manor during the thirteenth century. Ingelram de Fiennes was certainly rich enough. He purchased Gayton manor along with all the lands in the Honour of Choques, from the de Guisnes family in 1249 for £466 13s 4d. However, he improved the value of his land in Gayton by obtaining the right to enclose his wood in 1258, and sold Gayton manor on, separately, in 1270 whilst retaining the Honour of Choques. Fiennes, therefore, seems to be less likely to have had sufficient empathy with Gayton to have enriched the church, as this would not have increased his temporal profit, only his spiritual one. Any member of these families could have enlarged the church, and it is possible that we may never be able to identify the individual who was our benefactor, the occupier of the coffin, or know whether they were one and the same person. What we do know is that across the country, the rich searched for ways of investing their wealth to the glory of God.

Glebe land

In 1287 a convention which had arisen during the thirteenth century was adopted at the Synod (an ecclesiastical meeting) of Exeter. It put the finances of the parish church on a more formal footing. Either the patron or the parson became responsible for the upkeep of the chancel whilst the congregation was accountable for the upkeep of the rest of the church. No doubt with this in mind, Sir Philip de Gayton, patron 1297-1316, gave William de Gayton, parson 1304-29, the means to earn a living in the form of land. William received 10 marks rent from a burgage (tenure of land) which Philip bequeathed in his will in 1316 'according to the borough's custom'. This made the clerk more independent of his patron. He was now able to rent the land to a farmer or to farm it himself.

Adding a north aisle

In the fourteenth century, Gayton church was extended once more. It was an unusual extension because a north aisle was added, while the nave of the church was made smaller at the same time. The north wall, which became the north arcade of the church, was moved south by about half a metre, which threw the church out of symmetry. The quoins (large corner stones) which were used in the early church, can still be seen in position built into the west wall of the north aisle (see p2). These stones indicate the line of the outside wall of the original church. The result of this alteration is that the tower is no longer in the centre of the west wall of the body of the church, but slightly nearer the north side.

The north chapel

Once built, the north aisle was immediately extended to provide a chapel at the east end, alongside the chancel. This work was taking place about 1348 when the Black Death was cutting a swathe through the English population. Large numbers of the clergy fell to the plague as their work brought them into the homes of those that were dying. By studying the number of clergy that died, it is possible to compare the effects of the disease from place to place. Northamptonshire escaped the worst of the ravages, and as Simon de Veer survived as clerk from 1329 until 1369, Gayton may well have been relatively unaffected by the plague. This could explain why the extension to the north aisle went ahead.[6] Two tombs have survived to this day because they were incorporated in the building works. An early medieval coffin lid was used as floor paving and a small child's effigy was used as a building brick in the east wall. From the coats of arms on the end of the child Mabila's effigy, it can be deciphered that she was a daughter of Thomas de Gayton, from the lesser manor of Gayton, called Holt's manor, which disappeared in the sixteenth century; its location has yet to be rediscovered.

Mabila de Gayton, child effigy

De Gayton family chapel

Chantry chapels were built by well-to-do families to house their tombs and provide a place where they could employ a chantry priest to say prayers and obits for their souls, to speed them through purgatory. The architecture points to the extension to the north aisle being built as a pseudo-chantry chapel designed to house the de Gayton family tombs. Although no records to this effect have been found, four clues remain pointing us in that direction. Firstly, the chapel was completely separated from the church itself and it was not until 1827 that the chapel area became part of the church. Secondly, the only fragment of English medieval stained glass surviving in the church shows Philip de Gayton's coat of arms and, in 2005, it is on display in the north chapel. In addition, in *Northants Effigies*, Hartshorne suggests that the cross-legged oak effigy of a knight in the north chapel, appears to be the work of the same craftsman as that of William de Combermartyn's effigy, crafted in Alderton, Northamptonshire in 1318, and John de Hastings, 1313, at Abergavenney, and therefore is undoubtedly that of Philip de Gayton, 1316. The crossed legs were at one time thought to denote a Crusader knight but current opinion is that they were introduced as a strengthening technique by the wood carver. Without this, Philip's effigy would not have survived the rigours of the north chapel over the years. Furthermore, in the north chapel the earlier stone effigy of a full sized female figure is thought by Hartshorne to bear a resemblance to the Eleanor crosses which were erected by sculptor William de Ireland, 1291-94, and is of a good quality of workmanship; therefore, it is likely to be Philip's wife, Scholastica de Gayton who was alive in 1284.[7] The de Gayton family ruthlessly created a chapel chancel for their memorials using earlier generation's gravestones as building materials, but seem to have held back from creating a true chantry chapel and thus may have saved it from Henry VIII's attentions.

Seeking sanctuary

Until 1540 the church was not only a place for worship, but a place of sanctuary. Gayton church provided just this sort of refuge for John Atte Stile of Boxworth who appealed for sanctuary, 4 September 1351. This allowed him 40 days grace in which to appear before a coroner. Stile confessed that he had stolen a black horse valued at 12d and a bay worth 18d. When the case was investigated in front of twelve jurors, the communities of Gayton, Tiffield, Pattishall, Towcester and Cold Higham all had to be represented. These local men had to make an inventory of Stile's property, on oath, for which Gayton parish had to account: his property consisted of 5½d in money, boots worth 2d, a pair of spurs at 1d, a hood worth 2d, a girdle with a pouch worth 2d, a sword with a buckle valued at 4d, leggings and shoes worth 1d, and a lock worth 2d. Stile abjured the realm (he swore on oath to leave the country for ever) and Dover was assigned as the port from which he was to leave.[8] Gossip about this unusual incident would have spread like wildfire locally, but a moral was being learnt by the villagers, that this is what you could expect to happen when you stole from the rich.

The uncertain horror of death

Light floods in

In the late 1400s, when Gayton church boasted a nave, chancel, two aisles and a chapel, there was another flurry of building work, perhaps under the auspices of Robert Tanfield whose father, Thomas, was rector 1471-72. The nave roof was raised and clerestory windows introduced to allow more light to enter the church. A soaring chancel arch made room for the new developments in church practice. A carved wooden screen stretched across the chancel arch, cutting off the clergy to give them privacy, thus making the holy rites more secluded and mystical. The screen was painted and, perhaps, even decorated with gilded pictures of the saints. Traces of colourful paint can still be detected in 2005 despite the attention of Victorian restorers. Across the top of the screen there would have been a wooden loft and supported on this, filling the top of the chancel arch, there would have been an enormous crucifix, or rood, bearing the figure of Jesus with the Virgin Mary on one side and St John on the other. Above all this, the ceiling may have been richly decorated. In some churches a backdrop ornamented with stars and heavenly bodies was placed behind the crucifix, to eliminate light from the east window making it easier for the congregation to see the rood. However, this is unlikely in Gayton as the rectangular, decorated-style east window was not large and the new clerestory windows would have illuminated the cross. Either side over the chancel arch the walls would have been painted with a dramatic scene of Judgement Day, with Christ and his angels on one side, and the damned being prodded into a fiery hell by fiends with pitchforks on the other. This vivid illustration of what was to come must have haunted the mainly illiterate congregation. The doorway leading to the rood loft can be seen just above the pulpit, and the remains of the stairway leading up to it are visible from the south aisle. The rood loft itself was used to add drama to the late medieval services. Sometimes, the priest would give a reading as he towered over the congregation. On festival days, and particularly 14 September, Holy Cross Day, the rood would be decked with foliage and candles were lit on the upper part of the screen. The medieval screen is hidden away in the vestry in 2005 and has been woefully treated by previous generations, but it is almost complete. There is only one small panel missing from the screen, otherwise it would fit perfectly between the two sides of the chancel arch and is still the correct height to reach up to the doorway which gave access to the rood loft.

Marriage and monuments

In the chancel, to the south of the altar, is a heavily restored but very grand, sepulchred tomb with a large Purbeck marble slab which dates back to the turn of the sixteenth century. It is interesting to speculate to whom it may have belonged. The brass is no longer there but its matrix (imprint) remains in the stonework and indicates that it was made for a twice married man. Robert Tanfield, lord of the manor, son of Robert and grandson of

Thomas, died on 20 September 1504. In Gayton terms, he was a sufficiently important man to warrant a tomb of this stature and he had been married twice. The fact that the father of his second wife, Catherine, was Edward Neville, Lord Abergavenny, and Catherine's mother was Catherine, daughter of John Howard, Duke of Norfolk, would encourage us to expect no less a monument to Robert and Catherine. The size of the tomb enabled it to be used in the 1881-83 restoration as a divider wall between the chancel and vestry but it appears to be very close to where it stood in 1866. That it was not mentioned in earlier records may have been due to its dilapidated state and it has undoubtedly been heavily repaired, perhaps when the rector, George Butler, took over the responsibility for the chapel and its ramshackle monuments in 1827.

Purgatory

It is difficult to picture how colourful and impressive the church would have been when decorated for particular saints' days, such as St Margaret, St Catherine and Mary Magdalene, all of whom were popular in Gayton. Similarly, the church must have looked spectacular when decked out for the patronal festival of the Nativity of the Virgin Mary on 8 September. Everywhere, there were gilded pictures, colourful statues of the saints and Our Lady, and the scent of the foliage and the incense would have mixed with smoke from the candles and flaming torches. The flickering lights would have made the stained glass windows glow and in the distance, hidden behind the screen, the evocative, mystical sounds of murmuring would have been familiar, if not understood. In the twenty-first century we are used to a vast array of colour, smell and sound, but even we would have found it an awe inspiring experience. But there was a darker side to each service as the congregation, although unable to understand the words, were quite capable of interpreting the terrifying representation of hell painted over the chancel arch. They really believed that, whatever their fate, they were destined for a time in a most dreadful purgatory, and they were, as Francis Tanfield put it in 1558, 'perceiving and considering this transition life and fearing the uncertain horror of death'.[9]

Purchasing salvation

During the medieval period the church authorities encouraged rich and poor to give generously to their parish church, offering their gifts as a means of earning salvation with God. In the period 1499-1528, we know that those in Gayton who had sufficient belongings to merit a will left a bequest to the church. Because the prospect of spending a prolonged time in purgatory genuinely terrified them, anything which could shorten this future horror was welcomed, and so they responded enthusiastically. Those with money were keen to buy their way out of purgatory, and some ways of doing this captured the minds of the population more than others. Formal penances were performed and pardons granted, but people could also buy exemption from church law in the form of indulgences. The idea of pilgrimage became fashionable, as did the chantry chapels built by the well-to-do.

Intercession by saints or the Virgin Mary caught many people's imagination, rather more than the church authorities had expected, until as time went on venerating the saints began to look like cult worship.

Medieval package holidays

Oak effigy of Sir Philip de Gayton

Philip de Gayton, lord of the manor of Gayton, undertook a pilgrimage to the shrine of St James at Santiago de Compostela in northern Spain. On 16 April 1311, he received Edward II's licence along with letters to carry for his protection. Riding on a white horse was the traditional way for the well-to-do to make the journey to Compostela, the third most holy city in Christendom after Jerusalem and Rome. Pilgrims bought tokens which indicated the shrines they had visited. Compostela's token was a scallop shell which could be used as a dish or spoon when eating from the communal stews served to the pilgrims at the various hospices along the way. The Cluniac monasteries had popularised the pilgrimage to Compostela because pilgrims gave generously to their abbeys. Aymery Picaud, a monk, produced a book in 1139, the *Codex Calixtinus*. This book was a tourist guide for the pilgrimage industry which first told of the tales of St James, and then outlined the churches and shrines along the route, even describing the countryside and the people. Philip de Gayton would thus have been well prepared physically and mentally for his journey. For those not able to pay for adventures abroad, the shrine of Our Lady at Walsingham, Norfolk, was second in popularity only to Becket's shrine in Canterbury, Kent, from the fourteenth century until the Reformation. Both places became extremely wealthy from pilgrim donations. Joan Foster, another Gayton resident, left money in 1528 to enable John Ackett to go to Walsingham. Sadly, we do not know if this was on her behalf or on his own, or indeed, if he went at all. But it would have cost less than a major pilgrimage abroad, and pilgrims flocked to Walsingham to pray for salvation for their souls or miracle cures and they carried wax votive images of their affliction to leave at the shrine. Ironically, even Henry VIII made the journey.

I bequeath my soul into the hands of Almighty God

In an effort to find out more about attitudes to salvation, historians have looked at contemporary wills. Faced with death, testators traditionally made a statement of their religious beliefs in the preamble of their will, and gave donations to the church. However, this has to be approached with caution, as more often than not, the village parson was present at the death bed of his parishioners. He could also be present as an official witness to a will or even the scribe, and therefore he had ample opportunity to influence the contents of wills of a great number of people in his parish. Gayton was from early times in the Diocese of Lincoln and testators left money to the mother church of Lincoln; from 1541 Gayton became part of the newly formed Diocese of Peterborough and, immediately, donations were channelled to the mother church of Peterborough. This abrupt and immediate response was surely at the direction of the local priest. What seems to be the over riding feeling that comes across from the preambles of Gayton wills is that those involved were being extremely cautious. This is not unreasonable when the attitudes of the religious authorities were constantly varying. Changing times made testators nervous and careful not to say things that might be taken against them and their families by the authorities at a later date. Overall, the similarity of the wording leads to the conclusion that the parson of Gayton acted not only as witness, scribe and clerk, and was clearly fundraising for the church to the last, but he also looked after his flock and made sure that nothing was written down in a will which could cause trouble at a later date.

Intercession by saint or the Blessed Virgin Mary

Some early testators' wills that exist left money for the upkeep of altars or for lights to be lit to the saints. However, the affection for St Mary to whom the church is dedicated, shines through. The high altar was referred to by Joan Foster in 1528 when she bequeathed 'to oure blessyd Lady altar 4d'. There are two indications that an altar dedicated to St Nicholas was in existence from the late fifteenth century: in 1499 Thomas Chapelen left money to pay for a candle to be lit to the statue of Mary, near the altar of St Nicholas, as did Thomas Helys in 1519.[10] Interestingly, there are no references to money actually being left to the St Nicholas altar itself, although it must have existed 1499-1519. In contrast, there are four mentions of an altar to St Margaret: in 1527-28, Thomas Smith, William Foster, Thomas Wapul and Joan Foster all left money or barley to be used for brewing churchale to raise money for St Margaret's altar. Whether St Nicholas lost favour and this altar's allegiance changed to St Margaret, or whether there were two altars is unclear.

Candles blown out

Finally, the church authorities were forced into acknowledging that, although lucrative for the church, buying salvation was unacceptable. The 1536 injunctions, intended to enforce conformity and to discredit both pilgrimage and saints' cults, banned lights before images 'for superstition or lucre'. And from this date, Gayton wills no longer left money and goods, such as a strike of barley, to pay for candles to burn by the statues or altars of St Mary, St Margaret, St Catherine and Mary Magdalene. In 1540 John Creton left money for lights to be lit before the rood and sepulchre, both of which remained acceptable even after the second royal injunctions of 1538 which were harsher in their condemnation of the traditional cults.[11] From 1540-51 bequests were made to the church, the bells or the poor with only John Tarry, in 1545, risking leaving money to the 'high altar'. During Mary's reign, 1553-58, and the return to Catholicism, John Lyne's will returned to a Catholic preamble bequeathing his soul 'to our blessed lady St Marie and to all the holy company of heaven' but he only left specific bequests to the church in the format used by John Creton after the injunction of 1538. Since there are no further bequests it seems likely that the statues of the saints disappeared from the church between 1536 and 1540. From these wills it seems that religion in Gayton followed the church authority's latest instructions and, whatever the view held individually, no-one stepped out of line.

Not quite a chantry

Rich donors built chantry chapels and proclaimed their status by lavishly ornamenting them and vying with one another to produce the most opulent. It is no wonder that they attracted the attention of the avaricious Henry VIII. The dissolution of the chantry chapels in 1547 followed the downfall of the monasteries whose saints' cults and land grants had made them conspicuously wealthy. This crumbling of the Catholic infra-structure was bad timing for Sir Francis and Bridget Tanfield, Gayton's first family, who had accumulated sufficient funds to embark on building an expensive new manor house. Whilst some families in Northamptonshire, such as the Treshams, clung to the old religion and were openly confrontational, the Tanfield family were rather more cautious, but still reluctant to change from the old Catholic religion and embrace the reforms. However, the building work did give them an ideal opportunity to add a discreet entrance to their chapel by way of an underground passage. This lead directly from the manor to the door of the north chapel

Eighteen Tanfield children on a Tudor alabaster tomb. Note that one was originally forgotten.

which, although not a chantry chapel, and therefore successfully avoided being plundered, was being used in the same way. Francis Tanfield died in the last year of Mary's reign, 1553-58, which had seen a brief return to Catholicism. His deeply held Catholic beliefs were evident in the preamble of his will which commended his soul to God 'and to the blessed Virgin Our Lady Saint Mary and to all the company celestial'. He wanted his body, 'to be buried not sumptuously but seemly for my degree in my chapel chancel,' in Gayton church. The result was the alabaster tomb which has been conserved for the future as part of the Millennium celebrations. The incised slab depicts Francis and Bridget dressed in the costume of their day. At their feet, their eighteen children are clothed according to age and sex, each with their initial carved below. Infant mortality was high. Eight of the eighteen children died as infants and are shown in their chrysom robes, but the tragedy is intensified by one child being forgotten and added later above the others. In order that his tomb should be suitably housed, Francis left money for his executors to 'sufficiently repair the said chapel at Gayton within convenient time after my decease'. He then went on to arrange for obits (prayers) to be said for his soul, his wife, ancestors and children, every year for seven years. These were to be paid for by his executors and then, for a further seven years, paid for by his heirs. After the annual service the sum of 20s was to be distributed amongst the preacher, clerk and poor people of Gayton, which ensured a good attendance. It is a pity that we do not know if the obits were said or for how long, as Francis death in 1558 was followed by Mary's death and the return to Protestantism under Elizabeth I.

Confusion and change

Turmoil and tiny fields

Not only did the villagers struggle to cope with dramatic changes in religion, as did the rest of England during the Reformation but, at about the same time, Gayton had the additional upset of enclosure which totally reorganised agriculture. Life for the villagers must have seemed topsy-turvey with everything that they held dear disappearing. Change is seldom popular and leading up to the turn of the seventeenth century, Gayton experienced the greatest upheaval in its history. Not only had the look of the parish church altered beyond recognition, but the large open fields were being divided and hedges were planted around the smaller fields. With none of the sixteenth-century parish records available, we cannot judge how individual Gayton parish officers dealt with the removal of the Catholic trappings in Henry VIII's reign, 1509-47. The removals escalated in Edward VI's reign, 1547-53, were followed with an about-turn when Catholicism was reinstated by Mary, 1553-58, and culminated in complete change with the return to Protestantism in Elizabeth's reign, 1558-1603. From records elsewhere that do survive, we must assume that Gayton residents did as they were told and made the changes that were asked of them, when they were asked, just as people in most other places did. But it leaves us wondering what the 'man on the street' in Gayton really made of it all.

Beginning of the end

One of the first tangible indications of the changes, witnessed by the people of Gayton, was the arrival in 1552 of Edward VI's commissioners. They were sent around the country to make an inventory of all church goods and to confiscate those that were deemed unnecessary for the new Protestant services. Many churchwardens across the country, realising that they were about to lose their most treasured possessions, hid or sold whatever they could. The possessions of Gayton church that for one reason or another were not saved by Robert Brightwen and William Rogers, the churchwardens, ended up on the inventory. There were two silver chalices, as well as two copes, one of blue velvet and the other of white damask, and one vestment of white damask that Revd John Millys, rector 1544-80, must have been distressed to lose. The final item on the inventory, the church linen, however, was 'little worth left to the use of the church'. This statement is illuminating as it shows us quite clearly that the commissioners were taking things of value rather than acting on purely religious grounds as they purported.

Old Catholics give birth to new Protestants

How far the alterations, demanded during the Reformation, had been implemented in Gayton church is difficult to establish. The crucifix and rood loft probably came down in Elizabeth I's time but the screen may have remained *in situ*, at least until the Commonwealth period, 1642-60, perhaps longer. By 1611 the decline of support for Catholicism, and the rise of Protestantism in the Church of England had reached Gayton, and even the Tanfield family had lost the will to rebel. This was visible in the deterioration of Francis Tanfield's chapel chancel, repaired in 1558 and where, 50 years later, rain was coming in on the family tombs. His widow Bridget's death in 1583 probably signalled the end of an era. The younger members of the family had already made alliances with Protestants. Ironically, one of Francis Tanfield's grandsons, William Tate, born at the manor house in Gayton was to become a renowned Northamptonshire Protestant.

Samwell mausoleum

The new lords of the manor, the Samwell family from Upton, were faced with bills when they were ordered by the church authorities to repair the chapel chancel. However, to what standard it was repaired is not apparent. We know that this chapel was still completely separated from both the north aisle and the chancel in 1732 and used as a burial place for the Samwells. A faded sketch of the north chapel shows what must have been a tomb with two alabaster effigies, a husband and wife lying side by side, with other memorials presumably also Samwell tombs.[12] The north chapel remained in this dilapidated state until the early Victorian restoration of Revd George Butler. He opened up the chapel to the chancel and also gave access to the nave by way of a 'Tudor-shaped' arch. Funded by the rector, the area remained a chapel chancel. In 1968, Revd Orland, rector 1965-69, unhappy with his parishioners calling the chapel 'the Lady chapel', suggested that since the dedication of the church was to St Mary, then the north chapel could not have the same name. The Parochial Church Council agreed to leave the decision to the rector's discretion and he announced that the most appropriate dedication for the north chapel was to St Anne, the Virgin's mother. The community, with no close links to St Anne, appeared to be at a loss and from that day some have clung to the traditional idea of a Lady chapel, whilst others followed the rector's dictate and call it St Anne's.

Five crosses † † † † †

Injunction 28 in 1547 ordered the removal of altars. In many places they were quickly taken out, only to be searched for when Mary reinstated Catholicism. Where possible these earlier altars were restored and where no longer available, new altar slabs were made and dedicated. In Elizabeth's reign another injunction was issued in 1559 for the 'orderly' removal of stone altars. A newspaper article in 1866 about Gayton church, has the only reference to a dedication stone bearing five crosses being included in the buttress over the door in the north wall of the nave in Gayton.[13] Indeed, the buttress in question is a most unusual feature. The implication of these comments is that this slab was once the altar stone because it was marked with five crosses which signified the five wounds of Christ. It is not totally far fetched that the patron or church officers, forced to remove an item of such early importance as the altar, built it back into the church, possibly in the hope that they could retrieve it later. If this is the case, then the altar stone may well have been removed from the chancel in Elizabeth's reign. The buttress which partially hides the entrance to the north chapel could have been built during the repair work carried out on the chapel following Francis Tanfield's death. Perhaps it became important to the Tanfield family to be able to enter the chapel unobserved because they were fulfilling Francis Tanfield's wishes for obits to be said. It is also possible that the Tanfield family would feel a certain sense of satisfaction by secretly

North door to the church, partly hidden by buttress door

entering the church under the ancient altar stone. But this is speculation. Altar stones were inscribed with one cross in each corner and one in the middle and as none of the stones in the buttress appear large enough or have a suitable face visible, this remains unproven.

Communion table

In 1637 the Bishop of Peterborough's commissioners conducted a church survey to ensure conformity to Archbishop Laud's instructions that communion tables were to be railed like altars and communion was to be taken kneeling before the railings. In Sir Richard Samwell's family seat of Upton, where Edmund Morgan was vicar, this was resisted but Gayton avoided adverse reports and therefore must have been conforming. In 1643, all remaining altars of stone were demolished and the altar rails taken away. However, positioning the new communion tables now became a contentious issue. Some extremists moved them into the body of the church but usually they were taken from the east end of the church and moved to the middle of the chancel and covered by a cloth. This fulfilled the liturgical changes, making communion more like a communal meal.

Hokey-cokey font!

In 2005, only a wooden lid covers the font, but from 1236 more substantial font covers were compulsory and the holy water was kept under lock and key. This was thought a necessary

The font

precaution to protect the holy water from those wishing to steal it for use in witchcraft. A font cover, which is recorded in 1611 as being in a state of disrepair, was mended. However, 30 years later during the Commonwealth period, 1642-60, many fonts were broken up and simple pewter basins took their place. It may have been whilst being 'hidden' that the fragile cover disintegrated and the font was damaged. In 1662 the old fonts began to reappear in churches across the country and Gayton's appears to have re-emerged, as in 1682 the churchwardens were instructed to mend the font. Prior to Butler's 1827-28 restoration, the font held the traditional position for Early English fonts on the west side of the nearest nave pier (column) to the left as you enter by the south porch. In the 1827-28 restoration, the south porch was moved nearer to the west tower and the font was transferred to a more fashionable position, a little to the east of the belfry arch between two nave piers. Finally, the font was moved to the west of the south porch by Revd Williams Ellis, rector 1876-89, where a small baptismal area could be made, and where it currently stands. The symbolism of the font's proximity to the new position of the porch and the entry into the church through baptism is clear.

Triple decker pulpit

Protestantism demanded preaching and in 1547, and again in 1559, 'a comely and decent pulpit' was required to be set up in each parish church. There are clues that Gayton had no enthusiastic Protestants and reluctantly fulfilled this obligation as the pulpit dates from about 1603. This view is reinforced by a report that the pulpit had no cloth, 10 August 1611 and, again in 1631, that the pulpit and reading seat were not decent. Revd John Markes, rector 1583-1633, was by this time an old man. He was presented to the living by Francis Tanfield and continued as parson for 50 years, living through changes that may have been difficult to accept or finance. From a plan of 1827, we know that the pulpit was a typical Jacobean triple-decker having a reader's seat and desk for the parish clerk, as well as an elevated preaching level, which may have had a sounding board above. It was to the left (north) of the church, in front of the chancel arch but was moved in the 1827-28 restoration to the right hand side (south) of the chancel arch. In the 1881-83 restoration, only the pulpit itself was retained and its door was used to fill the side window.

Advertisement for John Taylor & Co, the bell makers

Ding, dong, bell!

Three bells and a sanctus bell

Bells rang out from church towers, such as Earls Barton, from Saxon times. The earliest mention of bells in Gayton is in 1516 when John Hunt left two strikes (or one bushel) of barley in his will, 'to the reparation of the bells'. Whether this means that the bells were newly installed and had not been totally paid for, or much earlier bells were in need of maintenance, we do not know. However, by 1552 when Edward VI's commissioners visited Gayton there were three bells of treble ring hanging in the tower and one small sanctus (saint's) bell hanging in the bellcote. This small bell, currently on the east gable of the nave, was rung when the Mass reached its most profound moment, to remind those unable to attend the service or working in the fields to join in and pray. In the south wall of the chancel, a window has been constructed low down. Although, in 2005, this low side window is inside the church between the chancel and vestry, before 1883 when the vestry was built, it was in the outside wall of the chancel. This may have allowed the bell ringer sight of the altar where during Mass, the priest stood lifting the host on high thus signalling the ringing of the bell. Revd William Gibbs junior, rector 1716-41, was either a devoted campanologist or behind the times. He spent £5 11s repairing the sanctus bell when the peal of six bells was introduced in 1726. The saint's bell, once such an important part of the Catholic trappings had been defunct for nearly two hundred years. In 1585, when Revd John Markes had been parson for only two years, one of the bells needed to be replaced. It is likely that the inscription 'Give thanks to God always', inscribed in Saxon capitals, was replicated from its predecessor. Similarly, in 1594, when another bell was replaced and the instruction, 'Fear God and obey the Lord', was also inscribed with Saxon capitals, it was probably reproduced exactly as it had been on the old bell. Such evidence could, perhaps, encourage us to consider these bells to be much earlier than the sixteenth century. Finally, when the third bell needed replacing in 1662 Revd Edmund Morgan, rector 1656-81, employed a modern inscription 'God save King Charles' and judiciously proclaimed Gayton's loyalty to the restored king, Charles II.

A ring of consequence

The three bells continued to hang in a tower only 40' 6" high. This meant that the bells were hanging almost level with the roof of the church and complaints were made in 1726 that they could not be heard from the other side of the village. The addition of a peal of bells was long overdue as Blisworth, Milton Malsor and Kislingbury had each had a peal of five bells for many years. William Ball, churchwarden, and William Gibbs junior, rector 1716-44, began an expensive tower raising project in 1726. It was an ambitious plan and the people of Gayton paid heavily for this luxury but change ringing was becoming popular and this would bring the bells up to date. William Ball was a good accountant and wasted nothing; even 'overplus metal, old clappers, old iron, and stones' were sold off. Even so, despite receiving many private contributions, William Ball still had to twice raise a levy of sixpence on the parish to pay for the building works. Why five of Gayton's bells were made at Rudhalls in Gloucestershire with the mark of Abraham Rudhall, bell founder, while the sixth was made in a different establishment with the mark of Thomas Eayre of Kettering, is not clear.

Bell cast by A. Rudhall, inscribed 'In Dei Laudem et Georgii Regis Honorem ex dono Thomæ Samwell Baronetti AD 1727'

The bell-frame

Bell benevolence

Thomas Samwell, lord of the manor, gave the first or treble bell plus the timber to build the bell frame. Revd William Gibbs gave the tenor or biggest bell (43 inches in diameter) plus £20 to the building of the tower. Even the churchwarden, William Ball, gave a bell and had his name inscribed on it. Harlestone stone, a term used for stone from both the Harlestone and Duston quarries, was used in the building works and a rope and gin were borrowed from Milton Malsor parish for pulling building materials up to the top of the tower. [14] Unfortunately the gin was damaged in the work and 10s had to be spent to repair it before it was returned to Milton. Thomas Wilson and Thomas Facer, the petitioners for the faculty and two of the instigators of this work, both had their land damaged and were paid 8s in recompense. An insight into how the Gayton men who were supervising this work became involved with the bell founders can been seen in the generous donation of 7s 6d to a man called Henry Bagley, (a name previously famous in bell founding), who was suffering hard times but had nonetheless taken extra pains with the work. Thomas Wilson was paid for the carriage of the bells to Gloucester and back home again and it is not difficult to imagine the celebrations when the welcoming party met the bells at Fosters Booth, three miles south-west of Gayton, especially as the churchwardens paid for the drinks there and on arrival home in Gayton. The bells were installed in 1727 in time to ring out in celebration for King George II's coronation, for which the bell ringers were paid 5s.

The life of a bell

The entire village was now able to hear the bells clearly and they rang out over the fields of Gayton for 100 years before major work had to be undertaken. The largest bell had to be recast in 1821 and R Taylor and Sons from Loughborough were employed to do the work. Another 100 years passed before a second bell cracked and Revd WF Stokes, rector 1920-33, and the churchwardens, JM Major Lucas and WA Ratledge, organised the recasting in 1931. However, this did not mean that there had been no problems in the intervening years. In 1882, the three largest bells were re-hung but the timber frame from which the bells were suspended was deteriorating and matters eventually came to a head in 1930. Taylor's from Loughborough had now passed into John Taylor's hands. He was called in to investigate the 'bad going order of the peal'. It was concluded that this was due to the defective condition of the timber bell frame and also the unsatisfactory state of the bell fittings. Gayton church was suffering from grub and death watch beetle. The bell frame timber which had been used and re-used in previous remedial work had finally come to the end of its life. A new, metal bell frame was essential and the cost was estimated at £295.

Communication, celebration and sport

Previously bells were rung far more often than they are in 2005; bells were used as a means of communication as well as celebration. Every village developed different customs and by 1898, a bell was rung in Gayton daily at noon; a pancake bell was rung on Shrove Tuesday; and a gleaning bell rung during harvest time. The death knell sounded if a villager died: nine tolls for men and six for women. Peals were rung on 24 May (Empire Day), 29 May (Oak Apple Day celebrating the Restoration of King Charles II), 20 June (Queen Victoria's accession to the throne) and 5 November (Guy Fawkes Day) for which the ringers received £1 each year. Ringing contests became a popular past time, perhaps even a sport, and Gayton was able to participate in inter-village competitions. Bell ringing has continued to be popular and throughout the twentieth century special peals were rung in Gayton. For Queen Elizabeth II's coronation, 12 June 1953, a commemorative peal rang out for three hours. In 1922, Grandsire Doubles were rung, a Cambridge Surprise Minor in 1961 and Annable's London Surprise Minor in 1992 and, of course, bells were rung to welcome in the Millennium in 2000 with Grandsire, Stedman, Reverse Canterbury, Plain Bob and Cambridge.

Parish work

Presentment of clergy

The gift of the advowson (the right to appoint a clergyman) was in the hands of the lord of the manor and traditionally he used it to provide a job as a parson for a younger member of a well-to-do family. This system stood for several hundred years. Michael de Northampton, for example, presented Philip de Northampton in 1270, and Catherine Trussell presented John de Haldenby in 1369. But when the Samwell family sold the Gayton lordship to an upwardly-mobile tradesman who introduced business principles into the appointing of a cleric, the county families were scandalised. The advowson in the hands of Richard Kent, a London fishmonger, was 'most shamefully put up to a sort of auction'. A wealthy young man, Revd Walter Griffith, bought the living and became rector 1753-93, immediately commuting Richard Kent's tithes into an agreed regular lump sum of £6 11s a year. He off-loaded his work onto the shoulders of a poorly paid curate, John Jephcott, son of Henry Jephcott, rector of Kislingbury.[15] The extent of Griffith's wealth can be judged from his property deals. In 1789 he sold land in Northampton Fields for £1,000 (approximately £48,000 in 1992). The land had at one time been part of St Andrew's Priory and was outside the town walls, and it was sold to enable a purpose built infirmary to be constructed for Northampton.[16] In 1805 Revd Griffith's widow, Anna Maria, died aged 90. She bequeathed 'her friend' John Jephcott £100 in her will for the trouble that he had taken in selling real estate for her, and gave £50 to Northampton hospital. Times were hard in 1805 and the £10 she left to the poor of Gayton to be spent on the day of her funeral, half in bread and half in money, would have been desperately needed by some. When Richard Kent unexpectedly died, his son, Major Richard Kent, was bankrupted and forced to sell the manor to James Hawley, a medical practitioner. Hawley disposed of the advowson, although rather more discreetly than Richard Kent. Nonetheless, he realised its value even with a present incumbent, by selling it in August 1765 to Sidney Sussex College, Cambridge, for £1400 (approximately £81,700 in 2005).

Books

The injunctions of 1559 required Erasmus' *Paraphase*, Foxe's *Book of Martyrs* and Bishop Jewel's *Apology* to be put in churches for the congregation to read.[17] Some parish churches, such as All Saints in Northampton, had considerable libraries. However, as late as 1611 Gayton church had still not obeyed the injunction and Revd John Markes was forced by the authorities to buy the *Paraphrase* and a book of homilies (sermons). Religious books printed in English became a necessity after the Reformation so people could study the religious texts for themselves. Everyone was required to take responsibility for their own spiritual welfare, and in consequence, literacy and Protestantism went hand in hand. These books were made available, sometimes chained to the reader's desk of the pulpit, for parishioners to read privately, in their own time. Books were prized possessions and those that owned them bequeathed them along with their lands and goods in their wills. Revd John Markes left his books in 1633, to be shared amongst the children of his son, Theodore, who was also a cleric; and James Markes, John Markes' eldest son, left his books along with his other goods to his wife Dorothy in 1643, indicating that she was also literate. The books belonging to Revd Richard Gifford, rector 1648-56, were itemised in his will and showed not only his high level of literacy and education but the depth to which he had studied religion. Richard Lockwood of Gayton House, left his books in 1696 to be divided between his two sons, Cutts and Richard Lockwood junior; and Revd William Gibbs, rector 1682-1716, left his books to his son, William, who became rector 1716-41. Books in seventeenth-century Gayton were treasured by the wealthy, and particularly by members of the clergy.

Revd John Markes, rector 1584-1633

Looking closer at Revd John Markes' will gives an insight into the life of a seventeenth-century cleric. Firstly, the preamble to his will is Protestant as would be expected in 1633. However, he chose his words very carefully which was probably a sensible thing to do, especially as tensions grew year by year in the run up to the Civil War. Next, he farmed the glebe himself; this was the land that belonged to the church farm. Markes was a sheep farmer and kept at least 40 sheep which he left to his son, James. Finally, although a farmer, at the same time he was very much the well turned out parson as he had two cloaks, cassocks and hats and must have cut quite a dash around the village!

Cleric and alchemist

But John Markes was not just a run of the mill parson; he also left James two galley pots and all his 'phisick stuff'. John Markes was dabbling in medicine. In *Religion and the decline of magic*, Keith Thomas says, 'The use of prayer was not meant to impede the use of medicine but to accompany it. It was as superstitious to rely on prayer alone, as it was impious to trust solely to physic.'[18] A man called Francis Anthonie, who had no training in medicine and was shunned by the College of Surgeons, had produced what he called *aurum potabile* (drinkable gold). Having confidence that gold in a drinkable form would cure all ills, those pursuing this goal believed that before the alchemist could produce the elixir, he had to rid himself of all vices. Consequently, the search for gold in a drinkable form became a spiritual quest. It was here that magic, religion and medicine became entwined. John Markes made up this 'medicine' from Anthonie's recipe and, starting with his own sixteen year old daughter, began treating patients.

Sir William Samwell

When the new owner of Gayton manor, Sir William Samwell, was seriously ill and his 'three doctors of physicke' were unable to cure him, John Markes was called in.[19] Unfortunately, one of the physicians, John Cotta, was a well known Puritan from Northampton. Whether Cotta was more infuriated at having his lucrative patient poached from him by a insignificant parson or having his patient 'cured' by an unqualified medical charlatan's 'quintessence' is unclear. Whatever the truth of the matter, Francis Anthonie exacerbated the situation in 1616 by writing a book, *Apologie*, in which all John Markes' patients were written up as case studies; the book included letters from the patients and their well wishers extolling Markes' success. Cotta was enraged, so much so, that in 1623 twelve years after Markes' treatments, Cotta wrote a book, *Cotta contra Anthonie*, in which he was scathing about *aurum potabile*, and berated Markes as much as Anthonie, and in verse!

> A gainefull trade you make Physicke,
> Thrive by the Divine and Chymicke,
> In two meerly you are carnall,
> And in but one spirituall.
> 'Tis two to one (we may feare it)
> The world and gaine choake the spirit,
> The gaine thus got, you backe doe owe
> From whence you stole it, and then you know
> A true Divine doth not well pray,
> Till that is stolne he first repay. [20]

Parish Clerk

Being parish clerk cannot have been a lucrative position in 1622 when Anthony Hurst was buried in Gayton churchyard, 'the parish clerk and a poor man'.[21] The clerk was a layman who assisted the parson with the service and the running of the church and Hurst had fulfilled this role for Revd John Markes. The long serving John Bosworth, who took over from Hurst, remained parish clerk for almost 50 years until his death in 1671. He had held the office throughout the Commonwealth period when he was, strictly speaking, the 'parish register'. William March, parish clerk 1739-56, mainly whilst Revd John Thompson was rector 1741-53, was paid 40s plus one groat (or 4d) from each cottager every year. There were approximately 42 houses in Gayton in 1732; therefore, his wages would have equated to 54s a year.[22] His duties included some heavier tasks that later were done by the sexton and as William March became older, his son and grandson, both also named William March, took over these responsibilities. Between 1749 and 1771 the church windows were cleaned regularly once a year and in 1761 a new broom was bought specifically to sweep the snow out of the church. It was customary for the parish clerk's wife to be paid for washing the surplice and also for mending it when necessary.[23] In Gayton's case, washing and mending took place five times a year. In 1764, half a yard of holland (a smooth hard wearing linen) and an ounce of thread were purchased for more extensive repair work which was undertaken by Mary Adams. William Adams succeeded William March junior in 1784, and George Dunckley took over the parish clerk's duties in 1832 until his death in 1855. Saul Saul, the village cooper, held the office sometime in the intervening years. He resigned in 1832, probably because his father died and he had to take on more responsibility in the family business. Dunckley had been assistant clerk since at least 1823; he was paid £4 a year in 1829 for teaching at the Sunday School and for turning the barrel organ handle during services. He had taken responsibility for the barrel organ from Joseph Clarke who was paid a guinea for his past services. Revd George Butler took the opportunity of the clerk changing in 1832 to sort out the finances and put the employment of the parish clerk and Sunday School teacher on a more formal basis, whilst also establishing a paid position for a competent person to assist the clerk and turn the handle of the barrel organ.

Churchwardens and churchales

Although a woman could be a churchwarden, and indeed was in some places, she rarely filled the role herself and invariably appointed a man to take her place.[24] However, there is no record of a woman ever being a vestry member in Gayton and the officers were drawn almost entirely from the body of yeomen and husbandmen in the village. Churchwardens had a duty to raise the money to maintain the body of the church and churchales became a traditional way of doing this. The parish officers brewed ale especially for the occasion and sold it with cakes or snacks. Before the introduction of pews, all the villagers gathered in the church, or in good weather and before the advent of gravestones, in the churchyard for sports, dancing, entertainments by minstrels and players, and other amusements. The heyday of these events was in the fifteenth century, when some parishes built a church house specifically for parish meetings and churchales. Perhaps the expression 'guzzle like a vestryman' had its origin in these events. In some places, the churchales became totally out of hand with all sorts of goings-on in the churchyard, causing the church authorities great concern. But churchales were popular with the parishioners and it was not until Catholicism gave way to Protestantism and, more particularly, during the Commonwealth period, that these village shindigs-cum-fund-raisers finally disappeared. Nonetheless, when Revd William Gibbs senior died, rector 1682-1716, an inventory listed his malt mill worth £2, malt chamber at £6, copper at £1 10s, pewter and brass at £20, and barley worth £8. These items may have been for his own personal use, but all this paraphernalia would have enabled him (or his son) to use traditional methods to raise money for the church, especially since amongst the outhouses in the rectory grounds was a brewhouse. Indeed, some years after his son took over as rector and inherited the malting equipment, the village embarked upon an extremely expensive project to raise the church tower. The demise of Revd William Gibbs junior, rector 1716-41, and the possible loss of the malting equipment for community use, must have been a blow. However, at about this time comes the emergence of an alehouse run by the Dunckley family. It is possible that demand for beer outstripped supply when the church stopped brewing their own ale and the Dunckley family benefited by adding a side line of brewing and selling ale to supplement the income from their carpentry business. In the following years a great deal of the churchwardens' money went on buying ale both at 'Mrs Wilson's' which was the Squirrel Inn over the road from the church, or at 'Dunkle's', the

Easter Monday April ye 7th 1740
The following Officers were
chosen for the Year Ensuing

Thomas Wilson ⎫
Thomas Marriott ⎭ Church warden
            Overseer of ye Poor
John Hiber ⎫
            ⎭ Constable
William March ⎫
            ⎭ Third borough

A Legacy of fine pounds left by
Mrs Gibes in hur Will to y^e Poor of
Gairton Distributed by y^e Oficers in y^e year
of ouer Lord 1739   5 0 0

y^e Disbustments of Tho Wilson
Churchwarden for y^e year 1740

pd for a paper as Gaue acount of y^e fast and pray 2
pd mr Whicher for a paper _____ 0 1
pd Coart fies and Charges at y^e Ester Uisitation
pd Tho Wilson for 2 Dosen sparoes ___ 0
pd Benans Boy 2 Dosen sparoes _____ 0
pd Joseph Mudaman 4 Dosen Sparoes ___ 0
pd tho Blunt 1 Dosen sparoes   0
pd Tho Wilson and Will Guins 3 Dosen sp 0
pd hart for a Dosen of sparoes _____ 0
pd mumford for a Dosen sparoes _____ 0
pd Tho Blunt for a Dosen of sparoes   0
pd benan boy a Dosen of sparoes   0
pd John Guyins for a Dosen of sparoes 0
pd Tho Wilson and will Gayins 2 Dosen spars 0
pd beanons boy a Dozen of sparoes   0

Churchwardens' accounts, 7 April 1740

alehouse run by the carpenter Thomas Dunckley's wife, Mary. Such purchases encouraged the services of the bell ringers and the workmen and kept the tradition alive well into the twentieth century. The Parochial Church Council (PCC) recorded, 5 July 1928, that 10s extra was put in the 'pot' out of church funds for beer money for the ringers and chimers.[25]

The vestry

The time at which vestry meetings came into existence may be disputed by historians and varies across the country, but certainly from the sixteenth century, the principal inhabitants of a village met together to discuss the management of ecclesiastical affairs, in a similar way to the manor court meeting to discuss manorial concerns. In Gayton, the vestry grew in importance as the manor's direct influence over parish matters weakened with the early introduction of enclosure. After 1600 villagers did not need to meet to agree on a joint farming approach as each could determine his own farming methods. Decline in the manors' influence over parish affairs necessitated legislation at various times in the sixteenth century which solved the problem of local government by imposing secular duties upon the clergy and churchwardens. The incumbent now had a responsibility to encourage his parishioners to contribute to poor relief and he was also involved in the control of 'rogues and vagabonds'. However, it was the churchwardens who shouldered most of the administration of local government because they had to care for the poor, maintain the highways and bridges, destroy vermin and organise the musters and the parish armoury, in addition to their chief function of maintaining the church and upholding ecclesiastical law. Individual officers were appointed from vestry members for certain responsibilities, such as overseer of the poor, overseer of the highways, constable and thirdborough (the constable's assistant). The overseer of the highway and the constable, however, were agreed by the vestry, but their names had to be put forward to the courts for appointment. It was not until the Local Government Act of 1888 that the work of local government was taken over by the County Council.

Live aid

Although Gayton's earliest records do not survive, the existence of a local man with responsibility for relieving the poor can be ascertained from wills of the period. Richard Burnell in 1564, left money for the 'overseer of the poormen's alms' to distribute to the poorest people in Gayton. In 1557 Richard Pacy left money towards the 'poormen's stock' indicating that the overseer of the poor's responsibilities were not only limited to collecting and giving out alms, but also for making sure that livestock was maintained, thus assuring the poor of a reliable food supply. The parish herd was in existence for at least 30 years, as William Green left 12d towards this form of poor relief in 1590. However, the cattle may have been allowed to run with someone else's stock as this appears to be the practice operating locally. Gregory Warren, in 1598, left his sister, Elizabeth, the choice of 'one sheep the best that she can choose of them that go in Thomas Pacy's stock'. As he was single and a labourer with no family to support, Warren was able to help his colleagues as well as the very poor: 'I give unto my fellowes Clement Tarry Henry Marriott Robert Walpul Mary Pinkard Katherin and Ann to each of them 6d and to every poor cottier of Gayton aforesaid 2d'.[26] Bridget Tanfield in 1583, generously left money for the poor in all the surrounding villages where her family had land: Northampton 40s, Towcester 20s, Harpole 10s, Kislingbury 10s, Milton 10s, Blisworth 10s, Tiffield 10s, Bugbrooke 10s, and Gayton 20s. She continued,

> I further will and devise that within one month after my death there may be a sermon preached at the church of Gayton whereat I would have all my children and neighbours of Gayton to be And at the same time to be a dinner provided for my said children and their servants as also for my said neighbours of Gayton at my cost and charges And I give and bequeath to the preacher 10 shillings And all the young scholars two pence a piece.

Bridget Tanfield was providing a nourishing meal in the form of a wake, bringing the whole village together, rich and poor alike.

Apprenticeships

Frances Samwell, widow of Sir Richard Samwell, found another way of helping the poor. In her will of 1678, she left £10 'to bind two poor boys of the same [Gayton] parish to some honest trade in London'. Not only did this give two boys, genuinely in need, a reputable trade but also settlement (a right to stay) in London which relieved the Gayton parish officers of the responsibility for their welfare and upkeep. Her provision benefited the people of Gayton twice over. Frances Samwell's genuine consideration for her staff is evident when, amongst what appears to be equally kind bequests to all her other servants, she provided generously for Francis Parker, 'my labourer', with 40s. Therefore, it seems likely that apprenticeships, especially when sponsored by those with connections, were sought after as she added the proviso that one of the two apprentices should be 'one of Francis Parker's boys'.

Almsground

Thomas Forman, in his sixteenth-century will left a yardland (a variable amount, but perhaps twenty acres) in Gayton field for the relief of the poor and in the hands of trustees. The responsibility of the trust eventually fell to John Pacy, Francis Gardener and Henry Brightwen. Only the latter was alive in 1613 to give permission for Sir William Samwell and twelve others to be appointed to administer 'the charitable and pious intent of the first donor'. Two years later, in 1615, the land was split into two plots, later called Little and Great Almsground, with ten acres in each and set aside for 'the general relief and behoof of the said town'. The first farmer recorded as renting the ground was William Southall in 1635, who had a twelve year lease on the land from the trustees for Gayton poor. Another deed, dated 24 May 1698, conveyed the twenty acres to ten trustees who were to employ the rents and profits for the relief of the poor. An Almsground rent book still survives, dated 1665-1756, which gives details of all the people who benefited from this money. In 1849, the rent of this land was bringing in £52 a year; the money was still being distributed to the poor who were not in receipt of parish relief, just as it had been from at least 1665. It was being distributed four times a year, in sums varying from 2s to 7s.

Poor receiving doles from the Almsground rent in 1655

John Ball	Martin Fowkes	Edmund Morgan
Thomas Brimly	Thomas Green	Francis Parker
John Brownford	Nicholas Hawgood	Thomas Sendall
John Burt	Em Luck	Widow Stow
Robert Cadman	Bridget Lyne	Francis Tarry
Widow Finton	John Marriott	

Churchland

When Gayton was enclosed in 1601, it was recorded by Revd John Markes in the parish register that:

> the 23rd day of March anoo dmii 1600/1 of Eliabeth Regina 43 it was agreed and concluded upon by the whole consort as well as Mr Francis Tanfield as by the rest of the freeholders and townsmen of the parish of Gayton that upon the agreement of the inclosing of the fields of Gayton into several plots there was a several plot set out and measured to the quantity of ten acres or thereabouts in lieu of as much as before lay in divers places of the said fields always accounted and used as town ground before time to the behoof and profit of the said town of Gayton[27]

In 1849 the rent from this land yielded about £39 a year and was spent on church repairs.

Almshouses

In 1836, eight small tenements or almshouses known as Brittain cottages (the spelling varies), were divided into two apartments each and were occupied rent free by the poor. Four of the properties were thought to be ancient and part of the poor's estate, and four were erected at the expense of the parish. Revd George Butler installed a pump for the tenants' use at his own expense, and he also paid for a window to be put into each house at the back to enable a through draught. By 1871, the need for this housing was evident, as all eight properties were tenanted. The four bigger houses were occupied by large families, and the four tiny cottages, with only two rooms apiece, were occupied by one or two people living in each of the two rooms.

Charitable concerns

The charities were causing conflict in the village by 1874 and many people were dissatisfied with the way they were being administered. Revd Nicholas John Temple, rector 1853-76, had been 'long confined to his room' and therefore was, as a trustee, unable to give the charities the attention that he would have wished. In addition, the nonconformists in the village felt that the trustees were biased against them as the doles were distributed in the church; a considerable number of the working class men of the village saw an opportunity to wind up the charities and receive a large one-off payment. An inspector from the Church Charities held an inquiry into the administration of all the Gayton charities at an open meeting in the school room in July 1875.

Church trustees

Due to lack of financial expertise, the income from the Churchland, which was used for repairs to the church, had decreased to £28 a year by 1874. Consequently the church was not being maintained to the necessary standard. Revd Temple had used £300 of the charity's money that had accrued to buy an organ in 1871. Such was the parlous state of the church's financial affairs that the inspector of the Church Charities' Commission was called in to investigate. Although it was agreed that it was best to leave the control of the Churchland charity in the hands of the rector and the churchwardens, the inspector pointed out that the present situation where there were only three trustees, one of whom was unable to fulfil his obligation to the charity, and one of whom was renting the Churchland himself, was far from satisfactory. He instructed the churchwardens on the course of action that they should take. After the financial reorganisation suggested in 1874, an improved income of £100 was achieved in 1894, and a church restoration instigated which ultimately was put into action by Revd John Clough Williams Ellis, rector 1876-89.

Charity begins at home

The Alms Charity was also investigated by the inspector from the Church Charities' Commission. The almshouses, supported by the rents from the Almsground, had also suffered from bad management combined with the trustees' capitulation to local pressure to hand out too much of the income from the Alsmground. This was given in individual doles at the expense of the upkeep of the almshouses. By 1874 the income had decreased to £40 a year: of the eight almshouses, four tiny cottages were untenanted, due to repairs not being carried out; and the four slightly larger properties were considered to be in a bad state, although still tenanted. The condition of these almshouses had become a divisive issue in Gayton. Mr Dunckley estimated that repairs to the almshouses would cost £290, whilst Mr Ratledge, a village builder, considered that they could be repaired more cheaply. The inspector rejected out of hand the demand by the labourers who were anxious for the capital to be distributed in small doles, and forced a reorganisation which improved the management of the fund. In 1894 the result was an annual income of £240.

Scholarships for boys

The inspector was adamant that small doles should not be given and definitely not to those in receipt of good wages. He suggested that the money should be used for the foundation of scholarships to help keep deserving boys at school. John M Payne, George Old a shoemaker, George Savage, George Dunckley a farmer, Mr Griffiths a farmer, and William Haynes a blacksmith, were appointed as additional trustees to the charity, thereby including some nonconformist villagers. On 12 June 1890, the committee elected Widow Lawrence, Thomas Cockerill, G Burrows and Stephen Middleton as pensioners for the remainder of the year and each was to be paid 7s a week by Mr George on behalf of the Alms Trust Committee. As for the almshouses, little was resolved and a deal was struck with the ironstone company. Four new cottages were built at their expense on church land to house some of the ironstone employees. When quarrying at the ironstone workings finished, the cottages reverted to the Alms Charity. The condition of these almshouses was still primitive even in the 1960s when compared with the eight houses in Hillcrest Road built by Towcester Rural District Council. The council houses were completed in December 1937 with piped water. Belatedly, in January 1960 the Alms Charity trustees had a water supply put into the kitchen of the almshouses but electricity was still only promised for the near future. In 1972 the four 'new' houses, still called Brittain Cottages, were sold by the trustees and Revd Denis Brown, rector 1970-89.

Allotments

Revd George Butler, rector 1814-53, was a great believer in self help; he was a keen supporter of the allotments and took delight in watching poor families cultivating their own plot of ground. At the time of the Charity Commission's investigation in 1874, there were nine acres of land let out in 70 allotments of about 20 poles each at the cost of 7s. The allotment holders wanted another 20 poles each and as land appeared to be available, the inspector moved on to 'other matters' saying that they should have it.

Noyfull fowles and vermyn

In an effort to combine two of their duties, relieving the poor and controlling vermin, churchwardens nation-wide paid set amounts to those who killed vermin and produced the heads of the various animals for verification. As a consequence, from 1532, dozens of sparrows (a term which covered all small birds), and many magpies, hedgehogs, polecats and foxes were killed each year. The churchwardens' account book was filled with the names of those who were paid, mainly children from poor families who were supplementing the family's income. The chore of verifying the creatures' death and noting down the money paid out was passed to the constable in the mid-1700s. [28]

Surveyor of the highways

For centuries, road maintenance was the responsibility of land owners who had to keep the roads in good condition at their own cost. Needless to say, this did not work and in 1555 an

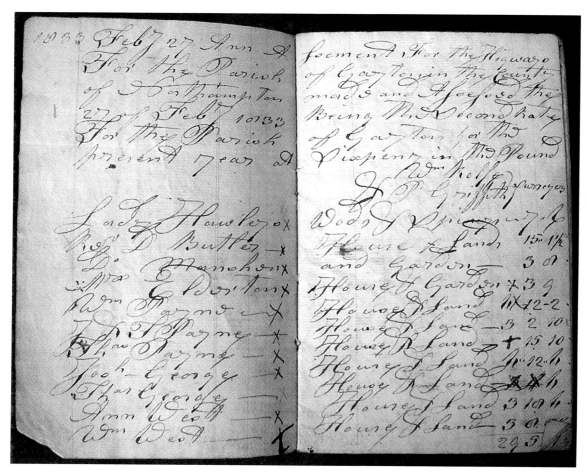

Surveyor of highways rate book, 27 February 1833

Act was passed which remained in force for nearly three centuries. Everyone was expected to work on the roads for several days a year, or else pay for a labourer to do the work in their stead. Parish constables received a letter from a magistrate who appointed the surveyor (or overseer) of the highways. Both the surveyor of the highways and the parish constable owed greater allegiance to the Justices than to the parish and vestry they served. In 1675 John Marriott, Gayton's constable, who was possibly also responsible for the highways, reported to the authorities that the highways and bridges were in good repair. But this was not the case in 1741; John Green was presented to the magistrates for digging a pit in the road between Gayton and Towcester and also for digging a pit in Mill Lane. The Surveyor of the Highways was not always the only member of the church to take an interest in the roads. Revd George Butler's daughter, Louisa, remembered being taken out by her father in his gig in the 1820s and then having to hold the horse for half an hour while he instructed a labourer on how to mend the roads![29] Gayton was ahead of its time when the vestry minutes record

Surveyors of highways 1803-1818

William George	James Payne	Joseph George
William Griffith	Thomas West	William Harris
William Payne		

in 1829 that employing the labouring poor 'upon the rounds' was 'done away with' and those that were unemployed were to be paid a daily wage of 6d to work on the roads.[30] The Act of 1555 was finally replaced by the General Highway Act of 1835.

Constable

The position of constable is an ancient one and it may be that in 1351, when John Atte Stile sought sanctuary in the church at Gayton, that it was the parish constable who dealt with the matter. In 1757 the responsibility for providing men, arms and horses for the militia changed from an individual to the parish. It became the constable's duty to list all the men in the parish liable to serve in the militia, and also conduct the ballot to decide which three men would serve for that year. This procedure usually took place at the New White Horse inn at Towcester and it became common for everyone to join together to pay substitutes to serve in the militia on behalf of the parish. The four militia lists still surviving for Gayton are dated 1777, 1796, 1798 and 1817. They record not only all the men liable to serve and their occupations, but also some imaginative disabilities that the men produced to avoid going into the draw. Whilst Gayton's constable was chosen from vestry members, he was appointed by and responsible to the local magistrate. However, he had a thirdborough appointed by the vestry to help with the more active aspects of the job. The constable provided the brains and the thirdborough the brawn. The latter probably came into his own when, for example, on 25 August 1838 a warrant was served on William Burton and expenses were claimed for taking him to gaol, whereas the constable was more likely to have attended the coroner's inquest upon Saul Hillyard, 16 June 1833.

Some parish constables

John Marriott	1675	Richard Cox	1741
John Hillyer	1727	William George	1777
Thomas Dunckley	1728	John Wheatley	1781
William Watson	1730	James Payne	1796
William Bowe	1731	Wm Payne	1798
Francis Baker	1732	William George	1814
Benjamin Dobbins	1739	Thomas Cockerill	1817
Thomas Hillyer	1740		

1799 Disbursements of Wm George
Constable for Gayton   £ s d

Pd Wm Middleton for Crows & Ravens   1 7
Pd Travell 1 Doz Sparrows   2
Pd Travill 3 Crows   3
Pd Hillyard a Foxes   5
Pd Thos Evins 5 Crows   6
Pd Middleton 6 Magpies   9
Pd James Phipps 3 Magpies   3
Pd Boddington 3 Crows   5
Pd Joseph George 5 Crows   3
Pd Wm Griffith 3 Crows
Pd the Charges Carring the   8
   Asessements of Land tax in
Pd 6 Single Turnpikes   3   0
Pd a Sessions bill & Charges   4
   Gave to 4 Saylors   1
Pd Wm Middleton 6 Magpies   4
Pd a Trampor a Hedgog   4
Pd Saml Dunckley 2 Magpies   4
Pd Wm Griffith 2 Ravens   2
Pd I Chamblin 1 Doz Sparrows   4
Pd J Griffith 2 Doz Sparrows   4
Pd Richd Rolfe 2 Doz Sparrows   4
Pd Thos Paine 2 Doz Sparrows   4
Pd Thos Watson a Fox   1
Pd John Griffith 2 Doz Sparrows   2
Pd Boddington 8 Doz Sparrows   6
   Gave to 2 poor men   2
Pd Pheasant Griffith 2 Doz Sparr
Pd Travill Boys 2 Doz Sparrow   4
Pd Mary Dunckley 3 Crows   6
Pd James Coleman 4 Crows   2
Pd Boddington Boys 1 Doz Sparr   2
Pd John Griffith 1 Doz half   3
Pd Richd Rolfe 1 Doz Sparrows   2
Pd John Boddington Magpy   1
   James Paine a Magpy   1
Pd James Lucy 2 Crows   4
Pd Pheasant Griffith 2 Crows   4
Pd John Boddington 1 Doz Sparr   2
Pd John Griffith 1 Doz half   3
Pd Richd Rolfe 1 Doz Do   2
                              £ 4 17 9

Constable's accounts, 1799

War and peace

Royalist rector and soldier

From 1633, Charles I and Archbishop Laud had been trying to impose uniformity on the church and to suppress the Puritans. In August 1642 things came to a head and civil war broke out between Charles and the Parliamentarians. Gayton found itself on the frontline in the war. The Royalists held Towcester (as the Saxons had before) and the Parliamentarians, Northampton (as had the Danes). The community took sides, thereby fragmenting the village in to different camps. A memorial plaque for Richard Lockwood, 1630-1697, of Gayton House states that Lockwood was 'educated in the warm feelings of attachment to the unfortunate, but exiled, House of Stuart.' In 2005 the plaque, sculpted by Robert Blore, is in the church chancel. Revd John Lockwood, vicar of Towcester, had a similar upbringing to Richard Lockwood and also had Royalist sympathies, as did the majority of the clergy. It was to his church in Towcester that the body of Revd William Burkitt, rector of Gayton 1633-43, was taken when he was killed in action after leaving his post to join the king's troops, south of Towcester. The life expectancy of the soldiers was considerably less than that of the rectors of Gayton, and Burkitt was buried by Revd John Lockwood, along with many fellow soldiers, 20 November 1643 in Towcester churchyard.[31] Towcester was abandoned by the Royalists six weeks later in January 1644 as they could no longer keep the town supplied. John Lockwood joined the Royalist cause and was wounded two years later at the battle of Naseby. He returned to Towcester to be replaced in 1647 by a Parliamentary intruder. [32]

Brothers at war

William Burkitt had been vicar of Pattishall, 1629-33, before being presented as rector of Gayton, 1633-43, and was succeeded at Pattishall by his brother Miles Burkitt. The two brothers held differing religious beliefs and between 1633 and 1641 Miles' Puritan views in Pattishall brought him into conflict, not only with Archbishop Laud, but also with his own brother, William, in Gayton. Many Puritans at this time lost their jobs and Miles was suspended whilst being investigated. However, ironically he was supported by William's patron, Sir Richard Samwell JP, of Upton and Gayton, who consequently lost his position with the Commission of the Peace.[33] In 1643, Miles Burkitt petitioned the House of Lords that he was oppressed by his brother William, who was then with the Royalist army.[34] Events had by now turned, and the Parliamentarians were in the ascendancy. It was now Archbishop Laud who was on trial, William Burkitt who was out of step with national policy, and Richard Samwell who was exonerated and reinstated to the Commission of the Peace.[35] The parliamentary commissioners valued the Gayton parsonage to be worth £140 a year in 1655. William Burkitt had given up a good living for his religious beliefs and his king, as well as ultimately his life. But with hindsight we know that he would have been in conflict with his patron, Sir Richard Samwell, and would have been eventually ejected by parliament for his religious views had he stayed in Gayton.

Appointee of the Commonwealth

Oliver Cromwell became Lord Protector, and committees were appointed to enquire into the conduct of clerics; many were ejected from their livings. The next appointment to the rectory at Gayton was not made until after it fell vacant with William Burkitt's death. Practically nothing is known about John Mackmath, rector 1644-48.[36] He in turn was followed by Richard Gifford, rector 1648-55. Gifford has been listed as an 'intruder', that is an appointee of the Commonwealth. These men often entered parishes throwing out the incumbent and destroying all the remnants of the old Catholic religion that had survived the Reformation. Richard Gifford does not seem to be of this ilk but he was rector at Gayton at a very sensitive time. However, since his family was closely related to the Samwells, his family ties and corresponding religious beliefs with his patron, ensured him of their support. An example of how things were managed in Gayton at this time of uncertainty can be seen in the circumstances that the parish clerk now found himself. In 1653, under the Commonwealth, the parish clerk no longer had a position and the village had to vote in a new 'parish register'. John Bosworth had been parish clerk since 1628 and the parishioners of Gayton stubbornly voted him into the new position which he occupied until his death in 1671. The procedure had been followed and the authorities were placated, but village life continued as before.

Suffering of the clergy

After the Restoration of Charles II in May 1660 the two factions, the Royalists and the Nonconformists, each produced evidence of the terrible sufferings that their churchmen had undergone, either before or after the Civil War. As far as Gayton was concerned, the Royalist supporters on the one hand, argued that William Burkitt was thrown out of his living by the Parliamentarians and replaced by an intruder. But this is not quite accurate as he was not replaced as rector until the living had become vacant by his death in 1643. Consequently, he cannot be deemed to have been ejected from his parish, although had he lived and continued as rector of Gayton, it is difficult to see how he would have managed when his religious views were so different from his patron; it is very likely that he would have been ejected. The Nonconformists on the other hand, maintained that Richard Gifford was removed and replaced after the Restoration of Charles II; but this is not the case either. Both Richard and his wife Ann died in 1656 and were buried in Gayton. Therefore Gifford, like Burkitt, avoided being ejected by dying at a critical moment in history. Revd Edmund Morgan's involvement is unclear but as vicar of Richard Samwell's family seat in Upton before the Civil War, and rector of Gayton afterwards, he certainly played a part. Further investigation needs to be done to unravel his involvement as his name crops up occasionally in Gayton before the Civil War, although he managed to emerge trouble free under Charles II.

Choir stalls and Commonwealth

Revd Richard Gifford's grandfather was Roger Gifford of St James Abbey, Northampton. His grandmother, before her marriage to Roger Gifford, was Amy Samwell, sister of Sir William Samwell who purchased Gayton manor from William Tanfield. Some have thought that because of Richard Gifford's connection with the abbey, that Gayton is likely to have obtained the misericords (choir stalls) from that great collegiate church through the Gifford family. However, it is difficult to see how this could have come about as Richard Gifford was appointed by the Parliamentarians. Across the country Puritans were destroying anything left in churches which they regarded as the remnants of popery: medieval screens, crosses, paintings, fonts, organs, service-books, vestments and stained glass were all suspect items. Whilst perhaps not holding extreme Puritan views, it would nonetheless have been out of step and extremely problematical, if not impossible, for Richard Gifford to be installing misericords in the church during his time as rector, 1648-56. Sir Richard Samwell of Gayton manor has a similar, if not closer connection to the devolved St James Abbey, through his aunt Amy Gifford (née Samwell) to that of Revd Richard Gifford, and Samwell had much higher social status. However, if it was not possible for Richard Gifford to be seen decorating the church with misericords, in the same way it would have been equally outrageous for Sir Richard Samwell who had been a supporter of Miles Burkitt and his Puritan stance. But,

The Three Marys, with beautiful foliage carving, is a unique misericord

whereas Revd Richard Gifford died in 1656 during Cromwell's Protectorate, Samwell lived to see Charles II restored. Times had changed. Following the Restoration, churches across the country were being refurbished and fonts were being restored to their position. Samwell may well have wished to play down his Puritan past, and it might have been expedient to offer the misericords to ornament the chancel for which, as patron, he was responsible.

Getting to the bottom of the misericords

However the misericords arrived in Gayton, and wherever they came from, they are not merely a local treasure, but a national asset. Misericords, or mercy seats, were designed for monastic and collegiate churches where services were long and arduous. The seat of the oak choir stall lifts up to provide a ledge on which an elderly or infirm monk or canon could prop himself, thus appearing to stand whilst actually being seated through the long and tiring services, particularly in the middle of the night. The underneath of these medieval seats was carved with a central subject and two supporters, one on either side. Due to the lowly position of this carving, (underneath the monk's bottom), it was originally regarded as an unsuitable place for holy ornamentation and it became traditional for misericords to be decorated in a profane and humorous, even lewd manner. To interpret the carvings it is necessary to appreciate medieval people's view on life and their beliefs. The upside down theme was usually followed, with much of the humour being centred on the world being turned on its head, or coarse absurdity to teach a moral.

Two unique misericords

In this respect Gayton's misericords are most unusual with four of them displaying religious scenes. Gossinger, in *The world upside down; English misericords*, suggests that Gayton's misericords may relate to mystery plays but the stalls are likely to have come originally from St James Abbey which is where the plays would have been performed rather than at Gayton church. The four with distinctly religious themes are: the Virgin Mary with foliage supporters; the Last Judgement with foliage supporters; the three Marys at the sepulchre; and Christ's entry into Jerusalem on an ass, with foliage supporters. The three Marys at the sepulchre shows an angel overhead telling the women that Christ has risen from the tomb, and supporters of a crown from which issue oak leaves and acorns. The supporters on this misericord are fine examples. It is rare for New Testament stories to be employed and the carving of the three Marys and that of Christ's entry into Jerusalem are unique. Of the remaining two, one is of a lion and dragon fighting, representing the traditional good versus evil story, but with an additional warning as the dragon is attacking a cub which is indicative of the next generation. And the other shows the devil, Tutivillus, who is frequently portrayed on misericords and would have been well known in medieval times. His job was to keep watch for a sleepy priest, or inattentive parishioners gossiping instead of attending to their prayers. He is dressed here as a fallen angel with only his hands, feet and the tongs (a part of which still remains by his wing) revealing his identity. The man and woman that Tutivillus is

Christ's entry into Jerusalem, a unique misericord

straddling are in church, indicated by the rosary they hold. The left supporter would have been recognised in medieval times to be a devilish beast, but comes across to modern eyes as fat and gormless! On the right is another devil with a writing tablet. He is writing down all the gossip and evil thoughts of the couple in church, put there by Tutivillus. The tablet he is writing will be presented against them on Judgement Day. This latter scene is very similar to a misericord at St Mary, Enville, in Staffordshire.

Colour and glitter

Early medieval English glass

Suspended in the top tracery of a window in the north chapel over Francis Tanfield's tomb is a small piece of early medieval, English stained glass displaying Philip de Gayton's coat of arms. The top of the border of the two lights (where the window is divided vertically) below the coat of arms is also early medieval.[37] The existence of such glass gives a further clue that the north chapel was built to house the de Gayton family tombs in the middle of the fourteenth century.

Flemish roundels

Following his restoration of 1827-28, Revd George Butler, rector 1814-53, wanted some medieval glass to decorate the east window. When he was offered a crate of medieval Flemish painted glass by William Henry Fox Talbot, a pioneer in photography, Butler was delighted. Butler had been headmaster of Harrow school and housemaster to a very unhappy Fox Talbot who was one of the pupils. Fox Talbot later became famous for his innovative role in photography, both in creating magnificent images and in their

Flemish roundels. On the left, the crucifixion of Christ, on the right, St Christopher

reproduction. George Butler called him 'my most admired magician'.[38] Fox Talbot was also a renowned scientist, MP and lord of the manor of Lacock Abbey, near Swindon, Wiltshire, which in 2005, houses the Fox Talbot Museum of Photography. Fox Talbot's uncle, Henry Petty Fitzmaurice, had procured 'some time ago' a box of painted glass from an old church at Beauvais in France, which he intended to use at his own country seat, Bowood House, near Calne, Wiltshire. In 1828 Fitzmaurice decided that the glass did not suit his purpose and he sent the box on to Fox Talbot, who in turn offered it to Butler for Gayton.[39] Butler accepted with alacrity. Some of the painted glass dates back to the beginning of the sixteenth century, c.1505-15, and Butler in thanking him said that it conferred 'dignity and elegance' on the east window of the chancel.[40] The roundel of the crucifixion of Christ became the centrepiece for the east window of the chancel; it was between roundels of St Christopher and St John the Baptist, and surrounded by more of the painted glass.[41] In the late Victorian restoration Revd Williams Ellis, rector 1876-89, moved the Flemish glass to the north chapel. The Eykyn family filled the east window of the chancel with late Victorian stained glass which they dedicated as follows: to Richard and Susanna Eykyn, who were Roger Eykyn's parents; to George Charles, 6th baron Vaux of Harrowden and Caroline (nee Vansittart) who were Mary Eykyn's parents. The lancet window in the tower was dedicated to Thomas Eykyn, Roger's brother. In August 1954, some of the Flemish glass was damaged and had to be replaced. As Revd WH Oliver, rector 1952-56, reported in the *Deanery Magazine*, this resulted 'from a gang of boys larking about'. The boys were taken to court and Revd Oliver tried to obtain Flemish glass from bombed churches rather than repair the damage using plain glass.

Powell's glass

Revd and Mrs George Kennard lived in Gayton Rectory to look after the parish for Revd Dr George Butler, when Butler made a trip to Boulogne in 1841. Butler's daughter commented that Revd Kennard 'had scarcely then begun to be eccentric' but he was no doubt ill and may have had to retire from full time work in the church.[42] Some years earlier Butler had purchased the tumbledown old Gayton House, which had deteriorated and was being used as a farmhouse. He demolished it and then rebuilt a grand mansion on a slightly different site on the estate.[43] In September 1841, when Butler returned from France, Revd and Mrs Kennard moved into the refurbished but still very new Gayton House. In 1847 Edward Pretty wrote in *Wetton's Guide to Northampton and its vicinity* that 'Mullions and tracery have been restored to four windows in this [Gayton] church and filled with Powell's glass at the expense of Mrs Kennard'.[44] This was only partly true. Mary Kennard eventually paid for eight windows in the nave of the church to be filled with Powell's glass.[45] In November 1846, August 1847 and May 1848, Mrs Kennard ordered windows to be made at James Powell and Sons (Whitefriars) for the nave of the church, paying £37 8s, £44 6s and £10 6s 3d respectively.[46]

Windows altered

In an 1801 etching of the north side of the church, all four windows were shown to be two light, lancet-headed windows with tracery and it seems probable that this was also the case on the south side of the church. One of the four on the north side is much larger and ornate, being a three light, lancet-headed window with flowing tracery; it is filled with Powell's glass paid for by Mrs Kennard in May 1848. It seems likely to follow, therefore, that three other windows, one at the west end of the north aisle, the equivalent at the west end of the south aisle, and another in the south aisle, were all made grander between 1846 and 1848. Two of the windows have three lights, whilst the other has two; all three windows have flowing

Engraving of the church from the north east, c.1801

tracery and are filled with Powell's glass paid for by Mrs Kennard. Sadly, as there is no early sketch of the south vista of the church showing all these windows, it is not possible to be categorical. Mrs Kennard also paid for Powell's glass to be put into three other windows that remained structurally unaltered but probably had been in need of repair work. George Kennard died in 1848, and soon afterwards Mary Kennard married Gayton's curate, Edward Preston Rawnsley. As Mrs Rawnsley, she continued making donations to the church.

Church plate
On 7 October 1552, Edward VI's commissioners made an inventory of all Gayton church property. They listed two valuable pieces of church plate, both silver chalices: one 'all gilt weighing 23 ounces', and the other 'parcel gilt weighing 8 ounces' (parcel gilt is the part gilding of a silver vessel on the inside). As neither of these silver chalices were included in the glebe terrier of 1635, which listed all the church property, it must be assumed that both were confiscated by the commissioners. However, at some time between 1635, (or more likely 1660 when Charles II was restored to the throne), and 1726, Gayton acquired three more valuable pieces of church plate. First, a silver lidded flagon weighing 40ozs; this is a valuable piece with an insurance value of £6,000 in 1991, and bears the Verney family coat of arms. It is inscribed underneath, 'The gift of George Verney Esq to the Parish Church of Gayton in

Northamptonshire' and has been dated to 1658. The donor, George Verney, was the brother of Mary Samwell, wife of Richard Samwell who inherited Gayton manor from his father, William, in 1616. Elizabeth Samwell, daughter of Richard and Mary, received an inheritance from her uncle, George Verney, which may have included part of the Verney family plate and the flagon. Therefore, it may be she who donated it to Gayton church on his behalf, as he does not seem to have had any close ties with Gayton church. Secondly, a silver salver or paten weighing 18ozs, with an insurance value of £2,000 in 1991, was 'The gift of Lady Elizabeth Langham to the Parish Church of Gayton Anno Dom: 1708'. Elizabeth Langham was the wife of Sir John Langham of Cottesbrooke and daughter of Sir Thomas Samwell. Sir Thomas inherited Gayton manor from his father Richard in 1673. The salver was probably commissioned especially for Gayton church as it was given soon after it was made in 1707. Finally, a silver chalice and paten cover weighing 14ozs, with an insurance value of £6,000 in 1991. This has no inscription and has been dated to 1570. As this silver ware was not included in the glebe terrier for 1635 it must, therefore, have been at least 65 years old when it was given to Gayton church.

Silverware

A small and delicate chalice and cover dating to the sixteenth century was donated to the church by Roger and Mary Eykyn of Gayton House. Roger Eykyn, as rector's churchwarden was heavily involved in the 1881-83 restoration of the church. It is possible that this plate may have been used for the first time at a service to celebrate the reopening of the church, when Bishop Mitchinson took a confirmation service. Another member of the Eykyn family gave a pretty silver spoon which bears the inscription 'Gayton church from Arthur Eykyn 1921'. However, it was not new when given and may be very old indeed as the hall marks are entirely worn off.[47] Another silver chalice and paten, dating to 1901-02, was given in memory of Revd Henry Marshall, rector 1933-35, and is the only one still used regularly at services. The church plate was insured for the first time in 1924 when the entire collection was valued at £80.

Arthur Eykyn

Disappearing candlesticks

More recently, brassware in the form of candlesticks, wafer box and vases have been given. A pair of Mesopotamian brass candlesticks were donated in memory of William John Wright, a school boy who died, 12 July 1926; and in August 1954, Mrs Boot presented a pair of brass candlesticks to the church. Anything of any value left in the church disappears and more recently Jane Pattison gave a pair of brass candlesticks to replace a pair of antique brass candlesticks stolen from the church. It is sad that in 2005 the precious church plate cannot be on show but has to be safely stored away.

Maintenance work

Liturgy and chancel

In 1681, Dr Morgan died at Kingsthorpe aged 67, having been Gayton's rector since 1656. He seems to have left a shabby, unkempt and possibly unloved church as the archdeacon made an order in 1682 for the chancel to be put into 'sufficient' repair. These day-to-day repairs of the chancel were the responsibility of the rector or patron, whilst the churchwardens had to raise the money to carry out maintenance to the nave. However it was not just the chancel that had slipped into disrepair but the nave as well. On 3 October 1682, the churchwarden, Thomas Stones, was required by the archdeacon to effect the repairs. He was told to repair the church windows, the north aisle floor, the seat by the reader's desk, and the south aisle seats; all the work was to be completed before 8 December 1682. Revd Morgan had been rector from the time of the Commonwealth and as an old man may well have had trouble adapting to the new order. At the same time as the repairs were being done, the new incumbent, Revd Gibbs, rector 1682-1716, with the churchwardens was instructed to buy a new *Book of Common Prayer*. This was twenty years after the issue of a revised *Book of Common Prayer* in 1662; whether the archdeacon ordered the new copy because the existing one was dog-eared or because the pre-1662 version was still being used, is not known. But if the services were irregular, this would highlight the decline that the church in Gayton had suffered.

Local tradesmen

The survival of the churchwardens' account book for 1726-1827 allows a close inspection of the repairs undertaken during this period. Although the churchwardens changed from year to year, they employed the same local tradesmen: the stone mason Thomas Branson, the blacksmith Ben Gibbs, the carpenter Thomas Dunckley, and the odd job man William March. They all lived in the village, with only the plumber/glazier, Mr William Wood, coming from outside. Ben Gibbs' blacksmith shop was close to the church, in Springs Orchard, halfway between Deans Row and the Manor house, right on the road. It was no more than a hundred yards from the church which made him a very local tradesman indeed! These men struggled year in, year out to undertake repairs made necessary either by depreciation, vandalism and the weather, or by changes in theology or fashion. It was the lead roof that gave the greatest problem and the most lucrative work to Mr Wood. He sent lead to a firm in Bugbrooke to be moulded into shape before completing the roofing work. William Wood also re-glazed the windows when either the weather or boys with catapults took their toll. Thomas Dunckley worked on the timber part of the roof, for which in 1742 he bought a nine foot beam. He replaced two church doors in 1744, and maintained the woodwork of the belfry and bell frame, even separating the belfry from the church in 1755. But Dunckley also had responsibilities outside, as in 1752 he bought 23 feet of new timber for the church gates, costing £1 6s 4d. It certainly appears to be a small quantity of wood for the church gates, posts and stile as specified, but no doubt he salvaged some of the old wood. It seems that he was working to a tight budget. Thomas Dunckley was paid considerably more for his work each year than Ben Gibbs, the blacksmith; but whether this means that a blacksmith earned considerably less than a carpenter or there was much less call on his services, is not clear.

Local materials

As well as using local tradesmen, the churchwardens were also getting their materials locally. In 1761 trees from the church ground off the Blisworth road, near Brittain cottages, were felled, transported to the church and made into boards on site. This was probably done by Thomas Dunckley. Again, in 1763 and 1764, he made use of church owned wood when trees were felled for church repairs; this time they came from the Little Almsground as well as the Church Ground. Sand, too, was taken from the Little Almsground. Thomas Branson used stone from Gayton pits. Village men such as Moses Moor and Samuel Cole were paid to dig out the stone and then to back-fill the holes afterwards. Only when necessary did Branson go further afield for his raw materials. He fetched bricks and lime from Greens Norton before Gayton's brickyards started up, and he used the better quality Harlestone stone around the windows.

White-washing

The passing of the old Catholic religion saw the disappearance of brilliantly coloured medieval wall paintings under a thick coat of white-wash which, from time to time was renewed. In place of the paintings, the chancel was sometimes decorated with texts from the Bible, the Ten Commandments or the Creed. When William Griffith, churchwarden in 1756, arranged for the church to be redecorated, his patron Richard Kent junior was undergoing financial difficulties. Kent's father had died, 12 October 1753, aged only 64 years, throwing the family finances into disarray because Gayton manor, including other Gayton land and property, had been acquired with a mortgage of £6,000. George Tymms of Harlestone thought Richard Kent senior 'would have discharged it with ease had he lived a few years longer', but he did not. Major Richard Kent junior's solution was to gamble. He borrowed an extra £3,000 to invest in a 'privateering scheme' but it was far too risky and he was eventually forced to sell the manor to James Hawley. It can only be concluded that Richard Kent junior, or his mother, agreed to the extra expense for decorating the chancel and chapel so that the grey marble tablet with its coat of arms, erected to his father, 'Ric Kent, Civis Londinensis' could be better displayed in the north chapel.[48] Robert Clarke was paid £4 for white washing the walls in 1756. In order to proceed with the job Clarke fetched from Northampton a quarter of lime costing 9s, three hundred and a half of whitening at 7s 10½d, two bushels of horse hair worth 1s 4d, an hundred of ham black at 2s 6d, 16lbs of glue worth 7s 8d, 7 quarts of linseed oil costing 7s, 12lbs of white lead at 5s, and two pots for 3d. John Snedker of Towcester was paid £10 10s for painting the church in 1756. This huge sum probably included specialist sign writing work as 30 years later in 1790, when some of the work was re-done, Robin Watson was paid for sizing and painting the walls twice, and for embellishing them with the Lord's Prayer and the Belief (Creed), and for drawing shields around the two. When the whitewashing of 1756 was finished, William March, sexton, was paid 3s for cleaning the church. A total of 15s was spent on ale which was consumed by the men involved with the whitewashing. Five shillings was spent during the procedure at 'Wilson's' (the Squirrel Inn), consumed by Robert Clarke, his men and William March, and 10s given afterwards for the ringers when the bells were rung to celebrate a good job done. The latter sum was spent equally in each of the two drinking establishments in the village. If the ringers were paid at their usual rate it would mean that they rang the bells on four separate occasions to celebrate the whitewashing of the church.[49]

Churchyard of Our Lady

Traditionally, testators requested to be buried in a 'decent' manner in Gayton's churchyard. A very early will, that of Margaret Trussell who died in 1441, widow of the lord of the manor, stipulated that she wished to be buried on the west side of the churchyard of Our Lady in Gayton. Medieval burials took place one on top of the other and the level of the churchyard, particularly on the south where most burials took place, rose higher and higher. This resulted in the church authorities declaring in 1611 that water ran off the churchyard and under the door to the chancel because of the 'highness of the earth'.[50] As soon as this problem was confronted and the number of burials stacked on top of each other was limited, more land was needed for the churchyard. Three extensions were added towards the east from farming land owned by the Hawley family: in 1817, 1952 and finally in 1967. But this was not the only problem associated with the churchyard. The report of 1611 also complained that 'the churchyard mounds are out of repair'. A wall was built around the churchyard but extensions to the mounds can still be seen in 2005 in the garden of the manor house and the old rectory, Wendover. In 1637 beggars were the cause of the problem. They had taken up residence in the church porch and were 'abusing and profaning the churchyard'. This concentrated the minds of the churchwardens and lead to a door being installed in the porch which kept the beggars away and remedied the situation. At the turn of the twentieth century, Gayton churchyard began to be known locally for its attractive churchyard. The Bishop of Peterborough, when visiting in 1906, raised its profile by proclaiming it 'one of the best kept churchyards in England'.[51] In 1945, with memories of the threat of death still all too familiar, the churchyard was still maintained to a high standard and described as 'delightful, with many kinds of bushes and trees and every path is bordered by a small garden'.[52] In the 1950s, skills acquired during the war for the more serious task of feeding the nation, were celebrated in many ways. An entertaining flower show was organised by John Hillyer and Mr Goosey, and later by Gerald Morgan and Eric White. Mrs Chester organised a team of ladies to provide altar flowers and Mrs Wakelin supervised another team of ladies, with a plot allotted to each, to keep the churchyard looking good. In 2005 we are fortunate to retain the headstones, each standing by its grave, which preserves the character the churchyard has had since the seventeenth century, despite the headaches it gives to those tending it.

Churchwardens that have served over the years

Robert Brightwen	1552	John Pell	1638	Samuel Maddock	1767
William Rogers	1552	John Tarry	1638	Thomas Wheatley	1771
Richard Burnell	1561	Thomas Stow	1660	Thomas Cockerill	1775
John Chitwood	1561	John Bosworth	1662	William Griffith	1775
Thomas Gardner	1562	Robert Cadwell	1662	Samuel George	1777
John Pacy	1562	John Markes	1662	Francis Maddock	1778
John Tanfield	1583	William Smith	1668	William George	1780
Stephen Atkins	1585	William Watson	1668	William Payne	1780
George Blisse	1585	George Reeve	1670	Thomas West	1801
William Houghton	1585	Rihard Caporn	1671	William Rolfe	1811
John Marriott	1585	Richard Fitzhugh	1671	William Griffith	1814
Francis Chappell	1588	John Markes	1673	James Payne	1814
John Chappell	1588	John Markes	1674	James Payne	1817
William Marriott	1588	Thomas Stow	1682	William Payne	1820
Richard Bailey	1597	Cornelius Gudgeon	1707	Joseph George	1821
John Markes	1597	Richard Wills	1709	James Payne	1828
Clement Pacy	1600	John Hillyer	1714	William Payne	1828
Peter Salter	1600	William Watson	1717	Benjamin George	1829
Thomas Marriott	1601	Thomas Facer	1721	John West	1831
Thomas Tarry	1602	William Ball	1726	James Payne	1833
John Tibbs	1602	Thomass Litchfield	1726	William Payne	1836
Thomas Cawcett	1609	John Markes	1726	John Harris	1841
George Hooke	1609	Thomas Dickins	1730	William Cockerill	1846
John Houghton	1610	Thomas Dunckley	1731	Thomas Payne	1846
Thomas Marriott	1610	Thomas Marriott	1737	Pheasant Griffith	1851
Robert Brafield	1613	Thomas Wilson	1739	Walter George	1869
William Southall	1613	Richard Ashby	1749	Edmund West	1869
Francis Jones	1614	Thomas Wheatley	1752	Henry William Wheldon	1870
Edward Houghton	1615	William Griffith	1757	Mr Kenning	1890
Richard Marriott	1615	Richard Kent	1757	William George	1907
John Lee	1616	Richard Hillyard	1758	Evered J Brown	1910
John Houghton	1633	William Morris	1758	EM Major-Lucas	1952
Theodore Markes	1635	Richard Ashby	1761	EE Barrs	1953
William Smith	1635	William George	1761	George Dixon	1958

Music, music, music

Sing me a song

In 1528, Joan Foster bequeathed the customary sum of 10s to pay for a trental (30 requiem masses which would be celebrated on 30 consecutive days) to be sung for her husband and herself. This task would have consumed a great deal of Revd Thomas Gardner's time. That Joan Foster intended that the masses should be sung rather than recited, may have meant that Thomas Gardner had a pleasant voice.[53] However, it is possible that Gayton had a curate as well as a rector, as Revd William Cory, who was working in the parish as curate in 1510, if still there may have taken these services. Or an unbenificed priest (one without a living; there were always more clerks invested than livings to support them) could have been brought in specifically to fulfil this request. Twenty years later, in 1547, trentals were denounced by a royal injunction. During the Commonwealth, music was frowned on and from the mid-seventeenth century 'lining out' became the practice for the 'singing' of the psalms. This required the parish clerk to read out each line before it was sung unaccompanied by the congregation. Parish clerks developed an excessively drawn out style so that each psalm took a long time. It was not until the eighteenth century that music began to feature in local church services. To start with, Gayton invested in a peal of bells. Some time later, hand bells were purchased or given to the church. In 1792, 1805 and 1820 the hand bells were repaired at the expense of the churchwardens. John Dunckley was paid £1 10s from the Church Charity in 1910, on behalf of the chimers. The organisers took their chiming very seriously; in 1926, two newly appointed chimers, Jack Chester and William Tomalin, were told that their attendance was not good enough and their services were no longer needed, although eventually Tomalin was given a reprieve![54] Hand bell ringing continued in popularity well into the twentieth century but by 1976 it had fallen out of use and it was suggested that the bells should be sold.

Minstrels

Very little is known about the minstrel band which accompanied the church services or when it was formed, although there is a reference for repairing the bassoon in 1810.[55] A more accurate date for when they were playing may be deduced from the building of a west gallery for performances. The gallery cost the churchwardens and Revd Christopher Hunter, rector 1792-1814, £42 4s 10d in 1805. What is apparent, is that by 1814, the minstrel band was severely disrupting the church services. They were quarrelling amongst themselves and their playing suffered as each individual played at a different tempo. Almost as soon as George Butler replaced Christopher Hunter as Gayton's rector, if his daughter's account is to be believed, Butler started tackling this problem. His solution was dramatic and taken without permission from the diocese. First he had to get his idea passed at a vestry meeting. Knowing that those who would oppose him turned up late to meetings, he forced a vote as soon as there was a quorum. Builders were standing by and immediately the decision was agreed, the minstrels' gallery was pulled down. There was no longer a gallery when the latecomers arrived![56] To compensate for the lack of 'musical' accompaniment George Butler bought a barrel organ which required someone competent to turn the handle.[57] Joseph Clarke filled this position for a while until George Dunckley took over from him. Later, in 1830, Butler had built at his own expense a two tier gallery across the west end, where he installed the organ in the upper section.

Organ music

Although hymn singing had started to be introduced in some places, it was not until 1861 when *Hymns Ancient and Modern* was published, that services began to acquire the form that is familiar today. In 1868 when Henry William Wheldon, an iron-ore merchant, moved into Rensbury in Baker Street, Gayton acquired a renowned musical talent. In his younger days Wheldon had been a chorister at New College, Oxford. Revd Nicholas John Temple, rector 1853-76, no doubt wishing to employ a talented volunteer, used funds that had accumulated from Church Lands to replace the old organ with a new one which cost £300 in 1871. Henry Wheldon took on the role of church organist which he held for almost 50 years. Music was a way of life for Wheldon and he did not confine his playing to Sundays. He used his music for the community in many different ways. Often he gave organ recitals in aid of various good causes, such as 23 May 1918 when the Northants Prisoners' Relief Fund received £4 2s 10d from a performance. Henry Wheldon died in 1920 when it seems likely that Miss Chester took over as organist. Miss Crockett became a voluntary organist in 1927 during the temporary absence of Miss Chester. In 1928 the organist's salary was increased to £26 a year which was Mr Anderson's starting salary in 1931. Mr Anderson was to be the next long term organist; he received a pay increase of £4 in 1936 taking his annual salary to £30. For this he gallantly cycled the 32 miles to Gayton and home each Sunday through the Second World War. There were three weeks during the war when a poisoned hand stopped him playing and an evacuee from London, Mr Jones, took his place. In 1945 the travelling became too much for Mr Anderson and for a time Mrs Fisher accompanied the church services on the piano. Mr Anderson celebrated 21 years of playing at Gayton church in 1952. He was followed by Ken Jeffs, who was also choirmaster until 1963 when Mr Major Lucas took over. Mr Evans was acting organist in August 1968 when Mr Duncan Faulkener took over for a few years. Miss Lucas, the post mistress and piano teacher, started playing the organ on a temporary and voluntary basis but was persuaded to take over more regularly in 1970 and continued sharing the playing with two men from Tiffield.

Woodworm worries

A major fund raising effort began in 1954 when Revd William Henry Oliver, rector 1952-56, launched an organ appeal because the action and frame needed a complete overhaul. This was due to the wood being 'worm eaten'; the cost of repairs was estimated at £300.[58] The appeal received a set back when the church was broken into and £2 10s was stolen

GAYTON

Rector: The Rev. H. J. Weller

CHRISTMAS, 1963. The Rector and Churchwardens wish all members of the parish a very happy Christmas. Last year there was some disappoinment that there was no service of Morning Prayer. For many years now Sunday Mattins has not been possible owing to poor attendance. Therefore Mattins on Christmas Day has not been held. This year the Rector proposes to have a short service of Morning Prayers with carols which will end after the prayers for the Church Militant. This will begin at 10.30 a.m. At 11.15 a.m. those who do not wish to stay for Holy Communion will be able to leave the Church. This arrangement should enable more parents and children to observe Christ's birthday in a manner He would wish by attendance at worship in Church. There will also be a service of Holy Communion at 8 a.m.

CAROL SERVICE. A nine lesson carol service will be held on Sunday, December 22nd at 6.30 p.m. Although the Church is still observing the season of Advent that day, perhaps this occasion may remind us of the spiritual significance of the coming festival so that we prepare our hearts accordingly.

WEEK-DAY SERVICES OF HOLY COMMUNION. December 17th at 9.30 a.m., 21st St. Thomas's Day, 26th St. Stephen, 27th St. John, January 1st Circumcision. and January 6th Epiphany at 7.30 a.m. each day.

DEANERY MAGAZINE. In order to make this magazine pay its way we would like to increase the numbers of subscribers. At present the Deanery is publishing it at a loss. In 1965 we may have no magazine at all unless we increase its income.

A VERY SERIOUS LOSS. After eight years of excellent but not very rewarding service as our organist, Mr. K. Jeffs, has decided to accept an appointment at a Church which is well attended. We are greatly indebted to him not only for the devoted work he did as choir master and organist, but for many helpful acts of kindness and good advice. It is he who saved us a very large sum of money by repairing the inside of the Church clock. We are grateful to him for all he has done for the parish. We wish him all happiness in his new appointment but greatly regret that he is leaving us. Perhaps these last few Sundays he is with us we might make a point of attending Evensong.

SIDESMEN'S DUTIES. December 1st Mr. Hyatt, 8th Mr. Robinson. 15th Mr. White, 22nd Mr. Rush. 25th and 29th Mr. Major Lucas, January 5th Mr. Cokayne.

PARISH REGISTERS

Claire Elizabeth Newcombe was baptised on October 13th, 1963.

Thomas Reginald Page died, aged 70, on November 13th. We offer our sincere sympathy to Mrs. Page and her family.

Revd HJ Weller's *Deanery Magazine*, Christmas 1963

from the alms box, missionary ship and an organ pipe which was being used for appeal donations. The culprit was soon found and received a five year prison sentence for his crime. The contract for mending the organ was given to Starmer, Shaw and Son and completed by 8 September 1954 when the organ was dedicated. There was a peal of bells and the flag flew in the tower and everywhere there were new acquisitions: the processional cross, the candlesticks by the side of the altar, and the oak table made by George Dixon, for the alms box to stand on. However, two months later a loan of £250 had to be taken out in order to pay the accounts and it was still not completely paid off by December 1955.

The altar with vases, cross and the two brass candlesticks that were stolen

Male voice choir

By 1877 Gayton had a well established male choir who wore surplices for the first time in 1883 at the service to commemorate the re-opening of the church following the late Victorian restoration.[59] George Dixon, the village schoolmaster, helped Henry Wheldon with the choir in the 1890s when the choir consisted of twelve men and five boys. In 1891 Edmund Roberts and Son, builders, carried out work costing £90 to provide choir stalls in the chancel. By 1907 the cassocks were in desperate need of repair and Mrs Annie Raymond (née Dixon) the schoolmaster's married daughter, did some work which 'made them look a little tidier' in the short term, and the Needlework Guild undertook to make new surplices.[60] The choir was rewarded for its service each year with various treats. A choir supper was popular as well as other activities including, in 1907, a gramophone entertainment by Mr Wheldon. The annual outing was, no doubt, a great incentive to join the choir. The destinations varied with a visit to Towcester in 1877, followed by the Crystal Palace in 1878 and over the years Northampton, Blackpool and Weston-Super-Mare all featured. The importance of the choir outing can be appreciated by the fact that school was cancelled, 9 July 1894, because of the choir trip! Certainly it was an exciting event, 17 August 1906, when the choir joined with the Conservatives for a day trip to Llandudno at a cost of £3 16s. Perhaps not surprisingly they did not arrive home until 3am. However, world affairs intruded and in 1914 the choir outing was cancelled due to the outbreak of war and was replaced by a visit to the pantomime later in the year. In 1921 the cost of the trip was borne by the Trust Fund. After the Second World War, choir trips were reinstated and in 1953 they went to the sea-side, this time to Skegness. For a short time the choir was under the direction of Mr Caesar who had moved into Rensbury following Henry Wheldon's death, and then Mr Major Lucas took over as choirmaster until his death in 1948.

Lady choristers

In 1921 a proposal was made to the Parochial Church Council that female voices should supplement the male voice choir. The women suffered a set-back when Mr Major Lucas won an amendment that they should only sing at festivals and special occasions. They were excluded from the choir stalls and seated less obtrusively in the north chapel. But the lady and girl choristers went from strength to strength as the male choir declined until, in November 1954, there was an appeal for more men to join to 'maintain a balance of voices'. In 1955 there were 27 robed choristers and later in the year the female choristers had hats to match their gowns made by Mesdames Marston, Markham, Hildred, Parr and Lansley. In 1958 the choir included Sheila Cokayne, 'Pem' Folwell, Gladys White, Sandra Jacobs, Avis Bevan, Rosemary Bryan, Linda Ratledge, and Blodwyn Bevan.

Music steals the show

Revd George Butler, rector 1814-53, managed to contain the rise of nonconformity in his parish whilst he was active, but as he aged he lost his tight control on the people of Gayton. A Baptist chapel was built in 1851 but the congregation quickly declined. In 1880 the Wesleyan Methodists took over the chapel but a split within the Methodists occurred and the congregation was approximately fifteen people in 1907. Henry Wheldon's arrival in Gayton must have changed the religious experience at St Mary's. His musical expertise was followed by the introduction of hymns and a choir. This may well have contributed to the fact that nonconformity never took a firm hold in Gayton parish as it did elsewhere.

Victorian solutions

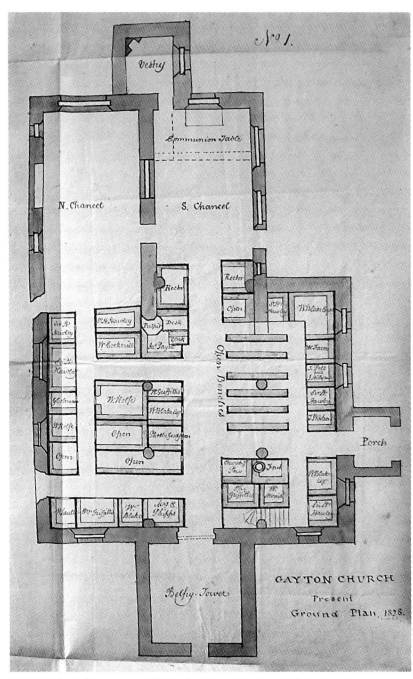

Plan of the nave c.1827, before Revd George Butler's alterations

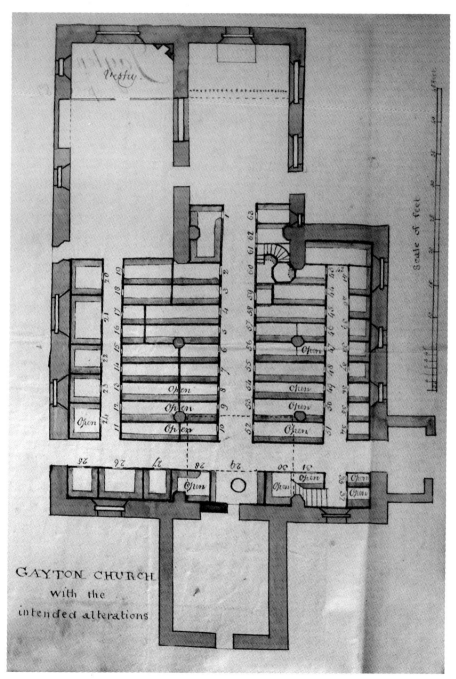

GAYTON CHURCH
with the
intended alterations

Plan of the nave after Revd George Butler's alterations in 1828

Pew rents

Churchales may have been frowned upon by the Protestants but, with the absence of a jollification, fund raising for the church became problematic for the churchwardens. In an attempt to find money for the upkeep of the church, a system of renting out the pews was introduced. This was to become most lucrative. Inevitably the poor suffered, as unable to afford to rent a pew, they had to either rely on their employer paying for their family's seating in the church, or sit on uncomfortable 'open' benches. Box pews became a status symbol for the well-to-do giving them privacy. The gentry and yeomen personalised their pews making them not only comfortable but even luxurious. John Markes and Thomas Wilson, yeomen, churchwardens and both successful men in 1744, had a faculty granted by the Bishop of Peterborough so that they could build a pew at the upper end of the north aisle facing the middle space. This pew was 11' long x 5' wide x 4' 6" high and tall enough to protect its occupiers from the draught. The church became a mass of higgledy-piggledy box pews and space was at a premium. When John Darker moved in to Gayton House, 1763-84, it was some time before he acquired a faculty to fit a corner pew at the east end of the south aisle, adjoining the east and south wall.

Early Victorian restoration

During the eighteenth century the renting of pews was often a contentious issue as everyone's status in life was reinforced by their seating within the parish church. Revd George Butler, rector 1814-53, dealt with the situation in his inimitable fashion. In 1827 he began his restoration of the church by removing the box pews in the body of the church and uniformly re-pewing the nave. In 1875 these pews were referred to as 'calf pens'.[61] Butler bought the wood from the old box pews to re-use in the chancel and it is possible that the linenfold oak reredos behind the altar may have been made from the old box-pew wood.[62] The oak reredos was described in contemporary writing: by George Baker in 1836, as 'elaborately carved', and in 1866 by Sir Stephen Glynne as 'modern gothic'. Later generations were confused by the re-used, old wood and Revd LE Browne, rector 1935-46, thought that the reredos was medieval.[63] Having removed the box pews, Butler was better able to reorganise the layout of the church. The font was moved to the back underneath two newly constructed galleries where the barrel organ was installed in the upper level. The interior of the church was paved with stone and the pulpit was moved from the north side of the chancel arch to the south. Several windows in the nave were enlarged or reconstructed. Butler had a false ceiling put into the chancel and the nave, perhaps to make the entire building a little warmer. This nave ceiling was ridiculed by a later generation who jeered, 'The nave was ceiled and coloured in a fashion more suited to a drawing room than a Gothic church.'[64] It must have been spectacular as the cornice moulds alone cost 12s 6d. They were made by a local man, George Dunckley. Iron columns were also constructed for the work and may have been used to support a mock-Tudor arch which opened up the chapel to the nave. It is probable that these columns were disposed of in the later Victorian restoration; one of them may still be propping up a farm building in the parish.

The interior of the church 1828-1881

A dilapidated state

The north chapel-chancel had been in a dilapidated state for some considerable time. Henry Hawley, lord of the manor, and William Blake, another large landowner, were very willing to renounce any possible claim to it and allow Butler to pay for all the necessary remedial work. With this freedom, Butler disposed of most of the tombs including many belonging to the Samwell family. Only the most ancient were kept and restored, such as the oak effigy attributed to Philip de Gayton. It is inevitable that we should speculate as to whether Butler used the monuments of the Samwell family as hardcore for his building work, as previous generations would have done, or whether they were re-interred in the crypt which, in 2005, is bricked off. Rain water, which would have had a devastating effect on any alabaster monuments, had been a perpetual problem coming through the north chapel roof. Until Butler installed spouts to carry the water away from the walls, the chapel must have been a very damp place. During these building works, Butler found the small effigy of a thirteenth-century child whose tombstone had been turned to face in to the centre of the east wall of the chapel and used as a building block when the chapel was built in the fourteenth century. A small building, protruding from the east end of the chancel had previously been used as a vestry. This was demolished in 1827 and the east end of the north chapel was separated off with the old medieval rood screen to provide a replacement vestry.

Church porch

The first mention of a porch was in a deed dated 1616. Legal proceedings such as signing a deed, were often contracted in the church or church porch to give the deal some consequence. In 1637 the porch was reported to be unpaved with no outward doors, thus allowing beggars to take up residence there. Gayton's churchwardens had to remedy the situation and they installed a single door that opened outwards and could be locked. The congregation from early times entered the church through a doorway situated at the centre of the south wall of the nave. When a south aisle was added, this doorway would have been rebuilt in the south wall of the south aisle where it remained, with the addition of a porch, until 1827. George Butler had the south porch and the most westerly church window in the south aisle transposed, moving the entrance much nearer to the tower and the west end of the south aisle. He employed Mr Keeley, a builder, to take the porch down and rebuild it. Butler paid the £20 incurred himself instead of the churchwardens. He also replaced the single outside door to the porch with folding doors. The church doorway appears much older than the porch because when the porch was moved the doorway was reconstructed as before. In October 1891 Edmund Roberts, the building contractor who lived at Fiveways, undertook the late Victorian porch restoration. By examining his bill for restoring the porch it may be possible to have some appreciation of how the porch looked in earlier times. A bill was rendered to Roger Eykyn, the rector's churchwarden, for stripping off the plaster, underpinning the foundations, pointing the walls, installing new roof timbers which were covered with Broseley tiles, renewing one stone and, finally, fitting new open framed doors with panels filled with open work and ironwork. The total cost was £42. It is unlikely that the porch walls were plaster clad in 1616. Knowing Butler's tendency to cover walls in plaster, it is reasonable to presume that the plaster removed by Roberts in 1891, had been more of a fashion statement in 1827, rather than a replication of an old style. However, as only one stone was renewed we can conclude that the porch is much the same size and shape as the original.

Sunday School

Bridget Tanfield's will of 1583 furnishes the earliest reference to Gayton's Sunday School, run by either the parish clerk or Revd John Chawner, rector 1580-83. To have a school as early as this in a small rural community is interesting, and it would have been responsible for the good level of literacy amongst the villagers. Much later, George Dunckley, parish clerk, ran the Sunday School from 1801-46. The Sunday School was supported by subscription and it grew in popularity. In 1818, 40 children attended but this had risen to 49 boys and 42 girls by 1833. Sometime between these dates, Dr Butler's children were brought in to help and the Sunday School was held in the Rectory laundry.[65] In 1829, George Dunckley was paid £4 a year for teaching the children and turning the barrel organ handle in church services. William Middleton was paid £2 12s a year for teaching the boys and Mrs Pell was paid £2 a year for teaching the girls. Even in 1907, the Sunday School continued to be well supported with three classes run by Miss D King, Miss Peasnell and Mr Prinxley, but its ethos had changed to be one of religion and entertainment, rather than religion and literacy.[66]

Church school

Very little change in schooling seems to have taken place between Bridget Tanfield's death in 1583, and 1801 when George Dunckley started teaching in Gayton's Sunday School. Until 1818 the Sunday School was the only place where any attempt was being made to teach the children of the parish. Sunday schools were funded by subscription and did not put any burden upon parents. This, therefore, encouraged poor families to allow their children to attend. Seventeen very young children went to the only day school which would have been more like a crèche than a school. However, by 1833 formal education had arrived in Gayton. There were three day schools in addition to the Sunday School: two were mixed sex and had about 28 children in each, and another, which opened in 1826, taught 25 boys. Children's attendance at the day schools was paid for by the individual parents. The increase in the numbers of those attending day schools is an indication of the way in which villagers had come to value education for their children. In 1846 Revd George Butler was the prime mover for the education of the children of the poor in the principles of the established church; he donated land and obtained the funds with which to build the Gayton National School in Dean's Row.

John Clough Williams Ellis restoration

Just over 50 years after the first restoration of 1827, there was a second remarkable alteration of the church. This took place under Revd John Clough Williams Ellis, rector 1876-89, Thomas Eykyn, curate, and Roger Eykyn, churchwarden, with the help of Matthew Holding of Northampton, the diocesan architect. Edmund Roberts and Son, builders of Weedon, carried out the work at a cost of £3,000 which was mainly paid for out of the Church Lands charity. When the faculty was discussed in vestry, those still loyal to Revd Butler, such as George Dunckley and Thomas Payne, put forward an amendment to resist changing the seating. But the wealthy modernisers, such as William Wheldon and William George, won the day. Not only was the seating changed but Butler's painted plaster ceiling was removed, the pulpit was refashioned and the chancel rebuilt. A vestry was added to the east end of the south aisle and the small circular window in the east wall of the south aisle was removed. This was one of the windows filled with Powell's glass which had been paid for by Mrs Kennard. The medieval wooden screen from the north chapel was set up to divide the newly built area into a vestry and a separate organ chamber. An arch was opened between the new vestry and the chancel and the early dresser tomb was re-set in the gap. Butler's stone flooring was taken up and replaced with hand made tiles, and wood block flooring was laid under the pews. The upper stage of the tower was renewed, the three largest bells were re-hung with new fittings, and the ancient arch to the tower was opened up. The remains of the old arch can be seen in the stonework just above this new tower entrance. The west gallery, recently created by Butler, was pulled down and the font was moved to take advantage of the space previously taken by the staircase to the gallery, near to the south door. The Flemish glass was removed from the east window of the chancel to the north chapel. The square headed windows of the chancel and chapel that had been altered by Butler were changed again. A large, spectacular east window to the chancel was constructed with a smaller, similar east window to the chapel; both were completed in the Early English style. Why the east window of the chancel remained unglazed at the time of the service to celebrate the opening of the newly restored church is a mystery. Similarly, it is still not yet known which stained glass manufacturer made a stained glass window donated by Roger Eykyn as a memorial to Richard and Susanna Eykyn, or when it was installed. However, at the same time a small lancet window in the west end was filled with stained glass given by Thomas Eykyn.[67]

Hot air

Heating the church has proved a challenge over the years and different generations have found imaginative ways of solving the problem. Box pews were built with high sides, not only to provide privacy, but to keep draughts from the worshippers; Revd Butler added a false ceiling to stop warm air drifting up into the rafters. With the demise of box pews and the removal of the plaster ceilings, as part of Revd Williams Ellis' restoration in 1881-83, an efficient heating system became a priority. The crypt was closed off with a brick wall and the remaining area was used for the installation of a heating system which operated on a hot air principle from Haden & Co., in Trowbridge.[68] However, the installation expense was not to be the only financial problem, as the regular outlay for fuel was a drain on resources. In 1910 the cost of coke was £4 15s for the year, one of the larger annual bills the churchwardens had to pay. Johnson and Wright, in 1921, were paid in instalments for the 'new heating apparatus' which they put into the church.[69] And when electric light was installed in 1929, it exacerbated the situation because it was now easier to use the church after dark when it was much colder. Yet another heating system was set up in 1936 in the underground extension of the present crypt. This time the McClary Pipeless Heating System was installed and twenty years later, in 1954, the boiler, flue and grid required a major overhaul. Finally, in July 1966, a Potterton oil fired boiler was installed whilst Revd Ernest George Orland was rector, 1965-69. In 2005, once again the fuel costs are rising and becoming a worry.

Twentieth century concerns

Before the First World War

Coming into the twentieth century, transport made the countryside more accessible as personal mobility grew. The design of the bicycle has changed very little since the 1880s when cycling parties started visiting country pubs. However, although the villagers were able to be more adventurous on a day-to-day basis, Gayton people were not yet pursuing their leisure time activities outside the village. They enjoyed an active social life within the church community when Revd George King was rector, 1889-1920. In 1907 there was an enthusiastic male choir and an energetic Mothers' Union, as well as a thriving Sunday School. In 1906, 43 boys and 24 girls were confirmed. The following year the numbers 'slipped' to 35 boys and 26 girls, disappointing the rector who was anxious to retain the male part of the congregation. However, the 1907 figure was still a considerable number if compared with 1952 when only twelve children were confirmed. Nonetheless, in 1907 one child, Bessie Hillyer, reached the standard necessary to receive the Sunday School prize 'for good answering at catechising'. The outside world frequently imposed on rural lives. Empire Day was celebrated in the school, with routine being suspended so that the schoolchildren could sing patriotic songs and learn about the Empire. Missionary work, both at home and abroad, featured largely for the church and the parish gave £5 13s 6d to home missions and £35 11s 3d to foreign missions in 1907. The latter included giving to those in India where the village had connections, such as Chota Nagpur. Revd George King's son went there as a missionary worker and his daughter followed later, travelling with her uncle, the Bishop of Chota Nagpur. But as always, the structure of the church could not be ignored and in 1908 the tower required maintenance. Liquid cement was forced between the stonework and the bell frame was renovated. However, some of the old timber was re-used in the reconstruction of the bell frame, storing up trouble for later. The clock, high up on the tower wall, which had been donated in 1848 by Revd and Mrs Rawnsley, was lowered to enable the belfry opening to be updated. The tower was crowned by crenellations with pinnacles and gargoyles in a last extravagant fling.

Mothers' Union

At the end of the nineteenth century local working class men were joining the Gayton's Rosebud Lodge, a branch of the National United Order of the Free Gardeners' Friendly Society and gaining a voice with the State. At the same time, the women of Gayton were forming their own branch of the Mothers' Union. As men stayed away from services so the church began tightening its hold over the community through the women, whilst at the same time making sure not to offend the men's sensibilities. Women wishing to join the Mothers' Union first reasserted their marriage vow to be faithful to their husband and then undertook to have their children baptised and to lead them to be confirmed. Finally, they vowed to endeavour to be steadfast in prayer, hallow God's day, worship regularly, and

Early members of the Mothers Union with date of joining

Mrs Dixon	1896	Mrs J Webb	1897	Mrs W Moore	1907
Mrs T Payne	1896	Mrs E Smith	1897	Mrs King	1907
Mrs Raymond	1896	Mrs Green	1897	Mrs Haskins	1908
Mrs E Ratledge	1896	Mrs Billingham	1897	Mrs Wm Ratledge	1908
Mrs King	1896	Mrs Tomalin	1897	Mrs E West	1908
Mrs E Cockerill	1896	Mrs Wakelin	1897	Mrs Randell	1908
Mrs Hillyard	1896	Mrs F Roberts	1898	Mrs C Moore	1912
Mrs J Hillyer	1896	Mrs Newcombe	1898	Mrs Rook	1912
Mrs Blunt	1896	Mrs Hancock	1902	Mrs J Haskins	1912
Mrs F Duckley	1896	Mrs Hammell	1902	Mrs Wright	1913
Miss Wootton	1897	Mrs J Ratledge	1906	Mrs Day	1913
Mrs Roberts	1897	Mrs Roberts	1907	Mrs J Payne	1913
Mrs Powell	1897	Mrs Puxley	1907	Mrs Hall	1913
Mrs Jas Hillyer	1897	Mrs Chester	1907		

Mothers' Union meeting at Rensbury in the 1940s

Back row: Marion Butcher, Mrs Thomas, Mrs Major-Lucas, Ivy Morgan, Mrs Wright, Gladys Keenes, Linda Kingston, Mrs N Paul, Mrs Bull, Mrs Wilkins Snr, Mrs Mansfield, Mrs A Webb

Middle row: Sarah Anne Hillyard (in chair), Mrs White, Mrs J East, Mrs Paul Snr, Mrs Folwell, Mrs Marston, Mrs Bridget Smith, Mrs Georgina Hillyer

Front row: Olive Billing, Gladys White, Mrs Hildred, Mrs Johns, Mrs Roe, Mrs George, Mrs Ted Cockerill, Rita Hillyer with Angela, Thelma Mansfield and Mrs Bull's daughter, Pam Mansfield and Nicholas defend their homes from the dangers of intemperance, betting, gambling, bad language, and other evils. During World War One, Gayton women took on jobs previously only done by men and they suffered the hardships of war as much as the men. As the war came to an end, so women over the age of 30 were given the vote. It is hard to understand, given the way they rose to the challenges of war, why in June 1918 the women of the Gayton's Mothers' Union were heart-searching over 'the great responsibility that the vote will involve' for those newly enfranchised women.

Mothers' Union banner decorated with Chinese lilies

Chinese lilies

During the Second World War, Gayton's Mothers' Union acquired a banner which they based on a Chinese design incorporating lilies. Perhaps it was not a coincidence that, 7 January 1936, Mrs Pakenham Walsh, wife of the vicar of Sulgrave, had given them a 'most interesting address' on Chinese women. Considering the circumstances of the Chinese women, it seems certain that women's rights were not concentrating the minds of the members of the Gayton Mothers' Union, in the same way that men's rights were concentrating the minds of the members of the Rosebud Lodge. Mrs Bull senior of Fosters Booth gave the material for the Chinese embroidery, and Mrs King of Chipping Norton undertook the first part of the work. The banner was dedicated on Easter Day 1942. Throughout the 1950s, the close-knit group provided a social refuge for all the new mothers of the post-war years. Church speaker after church speaker addressed the members although the rector, Revd Oliver, made little mention of either the Mothers' Union or their activities in the church magazine. By 1966, the Mothers' Union was in serious decline as its values had become outdated and, in 1970, the organisation was wound up. The outstanding £9 10s in the funds was used to buy a wrought iron pedestal for the church. [70]

War memorial

Paper and prisoners

The First World War changed the focus for charitable donations when church members looked for a means to help the war effort. The congregation participated in the national egg collections when Gayton's target was to send a gross (144) of eggs a week to Northampton hospital to improve the diet of wounded men. Waste paper was collected by the Boy Scouts each Thursday on their trek cart. They raised 1d per pound weight which went to the Northants Prisoners' Relief Fund. This job was made more relevant for the boys when the news broke that a scout, J Draycott, who had recently left the troop to join up, had been taken prisoner after only a few weeks in France.

Honouring the fallen

The church magazine announced at the end of the First World War, 'The committee appointed to arrange for our memorial tablet in the church have [sic] collected a considerable sum which will enable us to obtain a really good memorial'. In 1920 the war memorial was erected, made of Hopton Wood stone, and dedicated to the fifteen men who had died. Only one local man, Sapper JT Moore a Private in the Royal Engineers, died in the Second World War and his name was added to the existing war memorial.

The roaring '20s

Electricity came to the village in the 1920s but, time after time, the Parochial Church Council (PCC) put off the decision to have it installed. This was probably due to the expense at a time when the country was in the grip of a depression. In 1921 there were nearly a million unemployed people across the nation. Eventually, a faculty was raised by Revd William Fenwick Stokes, rector 1920-33, and the churchwardens, Joseph M Major Lucas and William Ratledge, on 25 October 1929 to put electric light into the church. On 31 March 1921, the PCC consisted of Mr Caesar, Mr J Payne, Mrs J Ratledge, Mrs G King, Mr Alfred Smith, Miss Ada Hillyer, Revd WF Stokes and Mr A Eykyn. Their major matters of interest were the choir, valuing and insuring the church plate for the first time, and cutting down four yew trees in the churchyard. The PCC appointed Fred Hillyard as sexton in 1922 at 16s a week but this was increased to 25s when the caretaker, Mrs Cox, decided to emigrate to Canada and he took over her responsibilities as well. Following Fred Hillyard's death in 1925, James Hillyer was asked to take over the role.

Moonlighting minister

During the Second World War, Revd LE Browne, rector 1935-46, continued as Gayton's rector rather than resigning to take up a new post as Professor of Comparative Religion in 1941. He commuted to Manchester University during the week to fulfil his duties there and this left him little time or energy to embark on projects in Gayton. Supporting the war effort became a parish priority and church matters were largely put on hold. On 1 January 1945, Revd Browne took a memorial service in Gayton to coincide with the funeral of Revd William Fenwick Stokes, Gayton's rector 1920-33, who had died in Buckinghamshire.

Revd Stokes and his family outside the rectory, pre-WWII

Remembering

It was inevitable that Remembrance Day in 1955, when the Second World War was still a sharp memory, would be an important community event. The report in the *Deanery Magazine* describes it thus:

> Remembrance Service was largely attended, not through any effort of the Rector's but through the backing given to it by members of the British Legion, who marched from Fiveways to the church, the Colours being carried by Mr E Cockerill, just returned from the Albert Hall demonstration and the Cenotaph Service at Whitehall – a great honour to Gayton through him being one of the three chosen representatives of the county. A muffled peal was rung under the direction of Mr W Eyden before and after the service as well as at the reading of the names of the fallen. The wreath was placed at the foot of the memorial by Mr Marston, Vice-President, and the Last Post and Reveille sounded by Mr Sam Cokayne. The Processional cross was carried by Mr Colin Markham; the Banner by Malcolm Cokayne, whilst the Rector was attended by two servers Robert Paul and Douglas Reid. The lessons were read by Mr LH Church and Mr RC Thursfield. The collection taken by Major Lucas and Mr E Ratledge amounted to £3 15s 4d in aid of Earl Haig's fund.

A roof over their heads

Housing became a post-war issue and Towcester Rural District Council completed their first post-war house in Gayton, 6 July 1946. This was one of two homes of the Swedish timber type, providing two Gayton families with a new roof over their heads. The churchwardens were a little slower to provide a new roof, in their case for the south aisle, but, 17 August 1948 ,the project was underway. Throughout the war years, church repairs had inevitably been suspended and now Revd Ivan Mavor, rector 1946-51, employed Norman and Underwood at a total cost of £1000. Half of the amount was borrowed from the Diocese of Peterborough but, so soon after the war, the parish had great difficulty in raising the other £500. The lead (destined to be stolen in 1970), was recast and re-laid, and repairs made to the woodwork, all of which came to a total of £581 6s 5d. It took years of fund raising and continual effort, and even so, it was not until September 1952 that the total loan was paid off. Only seven years later, it was necessary for Revd Henry John Weller, rector 1956-65, and churchwardens, Edward Major Lucas and George Dixon, to request another faculty for more repairs to the church roof, this time to replace damaged timbers and treat woodworm and death watch beetle. Timbers in the nave roof, which had been re-used rather than replaced in other renovations, had 'a considerable amount of death watch beetle'.

A new rectory

Revd William Henry Oliver whilst curate-in-charge, worked to resolve the problem of the accommodation for Gayton's clergy. The old rectory was large and a drain on limited church resources. Frustrated, Revd Oliver managed to do battle with church bureaucracy, sell the old rectory and achieve the building of a modern, more easily maintainable house. He reported in the church magazine in October 1952, 'I am afraid the laity have no idea how expensive, long-winded and out-of-date much of our ecclesiastical machinery is'; a sentiment which some in the village could no doubt relate to even now! Revd Oliver, rector 1952-56, was the first to hold the benefices of Gayton and Tiffield in plurality from 23 November 1951, and in union from 23 June 1953.[71]

Children's corner

After the war, as things returned to normal, the birth rate went up. This increase in the number of births nationally, which later generations described as 'the bulge', was mirrored in a rise in the number of baptisms as the church reflected contemporary preoccupations. The emphasis was on the young, and a children's corner was set aside in the church and decorated with pictures and books. In an effort to improve the furnishings in the church Revd Oliver, rector 1952-56, oversaw a project to cover the walls behind the font with new baptistry curtains in memory of a former rector, Revd Henry Marshall, rector 1933-35. Marshall in 1935, had taken down the previous curtains because they were in a 'dilapidated state'. The new curtains were made by Mesdames Morgan, Billing, Hildred and Rogers and were funded with donations from those commemorating their own, their children or their grandchildren's baptism. The curtains were dedicated at the Patronal Festival, 8 September 1955. 'Make do and mend', a byword from the war, was put aside and altar linen, frontals, vestments and choir robes were renewed by the Embroidery and Sewing Guild which met every month at the Rectory. The north chapel also had new service books, altar coverings and curtains; the brass tablet to commemorate William Houghton who died in 1600, was re-plated by George Dixon.

Major repairs

Revd Ernest George Orland, rector 1965-69, was an active member of the diocese: he played cricket for the diocesan clergy team and was president of the Peterborough Diocesan Guild of Church Bell Ringers. He needed all his energy to cope with his new parish. Lack of money had limited the maintenance projects that could be taken on after the Second World War, but the architect's report of 1966 highlighted how much structural work needed to be done. There was dry rot in the nave roof, the finials and the access cover at the top of the tower needed repair work, the windows' stonework, glazing and metalwork was poor, the guttering needed attention, the existing electrics needed updating, and the wood floor and timber bearers needed replacing. Revd Orland was overwhelmed with work, but although unable to put everything right immediately, he set about fund raising

Baptisms commemorated by a gift to the Baptistry Curtain Fund in 1955

Diana Jane Arkell
Pearl Daphne Billing
Aubrey Chester
Mary Constance Chester
Christine Joyce Cockerill
Michael John Cockerill
John Edward Cokayne
Pamela Maureen Cokayne
Hugh Leonard Crossley
George Dixon
Roger Eykyn
Julia Helen Gable
Nicholas Gordon
Trevor Green
Angela Rosa Hillier
Beryl Georgina May Keenes
Vivian Irene Kingston
Wendy Bertha Morgan
Gerald Howard Payne Morgan
Helen Vera Parish
Margaret Jane Parish

Susan Mary Payne
Maurice Payne
Yvonne Dawn Pirie
Carol Rosalyn Pirie
Elizabeth Ann Ratledge
John Edgar Paul Ratledge
Joseph Frederick Bryan Ratledge
Howard James Nevill Ratledge
William Ernest Peter Ratledge
Anthony Jeffery Ratledge
Terence Edwin George Ratledge
Verina Jean Ratledge
Elaine Winifred Ratledge
Linda Josephine Ratledge
Valerie Ann Reid
Rosalyn Anne Rogers
John Anthony Rogers
Hazel June Shipperley
Avis Jean Thomas
Shirley West
Peter Alan Wilkins

and dealing with the most urgent matters. His experience as an engineering draughtsman must have helped. Besides installing a new heating system and a fresh cold water supply, the churchyard wall was patched up, loose portions of the tower pinnacles were removed, and some stonework around the windows was replaced with Welton stone, a local calcareous ironstone. The church doors and the seat in the porch were repaired. The wood, which had been a continual problem, was once again giving cause for anxiety. It could not be ignored and the wood block flooring and timber bearers under the pews were renewed. But only ten years later, in March 1978, further measures had to be undertaken to save the woodwork; an infestation of death watch beetle and woodworm was treated by fumigation. It is not evident to which windows the glazier was referring when he ventured his opinion that the 'existing glass has few meritorious qualities and modern clear glass would be preferable' and he also warned that replacements of the coloured glass could not be made exactly.[72] It may be that he was referring to the vestry windows which were ultimately repaired with nine panes of glass found in the tower. An existing altar table was moved from the north chapel to the south aisle, with another of George Dixon's wooden tables being

71

used as an altar table in the north chapel. Revd Orland's concerns were not just focused on the structure; for liturgical purposes an aumbrey (cupboard) was put into the wall of the sanctuary enabling communion to be consecrated on Sunday and retained until later in the week.

Changing times

In 1973 although there were 103 names on the electoral roll, trends that would continue throughout the second half of the twentieth century were beginning to be recognised. There was a 'falling off in attendance at the children's services' and the choir numbers were down, particularly the men. Also, an interesting change in attitude was taking place; Revd Denis Brown, rector 1970-89, commented in 1975 that 'there was no reason why lady sidesmen should not serve and volunteers from the fair sex would be most welcome'. A year later, there were two female sidesmen, Miss Goodyer and Miss Wakelin and by 1977 the PCC were calling them 'sidespersons'.

Clock and tower

In the 1973 election to the PCC, there was a unanimous vote for Mrs Burleigh, Mrs Green, Mrs Goodyer, Mrs Major Lucas, Mrs Rogers, Mr Allen, Mr Briglin, Mr Goodyer, Mr Schanschieff, Mr Smith and three ex-officio members, Mr Major Lucas, Mr Watterson and Mr White. Their first task was to initiate work on the church tower. The 1966 faculty was extended to 1974 and Messrs Crow were instructed to carry out the repairs at a cost of £3,365 plus VAT. Rowie Parish had been working voluntarily with Tony, Philip and David Ratledge to electrify the clock winding system, and the clock face was painted whilst the scaffolding for the tower work was still in place. Fund raising to pay for the work on the tower became vital and some interesting ideas were discussed: Mr Spencer Gunn would be asked to put on an exhibition of his collection of musical boxes and early gramophones, a Gilbert and Sullivan evening was proposed, and an auction combined with a sweepstake on the Grand National was thought to be a great attraction if accompanied by a colour television in the village hall. The last suggestion was thought to be too difficult for both economic and technical reasons. For several years the church fete was held in the grounds of the Dower House in Spring and then alternated with an Autumn fair.

Presentations

The PCC occasionally acknowledged the contribution of exceptionally dedicated church workers. They arranged the presentation of a clock to Ted Cockerill, sexton, whose ill health was preventing him from mowing the churchyard. The clock was given to Ted and his wife on the occasion of their golden wedding anniversary, 27 September 1973, and a wreath of flowers was sent when his funeral took place, 24 January 1977. In 1976, when the 'Vicar's Warden for about thirty years', Edward Major Lucas left the village, a joint collection with the Parish Council was made for him and his wife.

Festivals and funerals

The first flower festival was held 5 and 6 July 1980, and organised by Mrs Gwen Crossley, Mrs Sandra Pennock and Mrs Jane Pattison. It was a great triumph, so much so, that flower festivals were held annually for many years. They took place in late June, and in 1983, the festival raised an amazing £1,600. Although the profit varied, it was for a while a most successful fund raiser. New exciting ideas were discussed for inclusion in the event: Mrs Schanschieff was asked if she would display her collection of christening gowns, Michael East his new milking parlour, and Glyn Evans his paintings. A tug-of-war was suggested and it was agreed that this would be acceptable as long as there was no beer tent! But life continued, not always so happily; a request was received in 1986 from Mr Noble, who worked for Sir John Palmer Ltd who had built St Mary's Court in 1974, for him and his wife to be buried at the foot of their daughter's grave in the churchyard and a faculty was raised. Another sad time was recognised, this time for both Revd Dr Brown, rector 1970-89, and the parish. An oak screen was made by woodcarver Mr L Goff of Pury's End in 1984. This filled the arch leading from the nave to the tower and was in memory of Canon Brown's wife, Leonara Marjorie, who died in 1977, and his daughter, Gwendoline, who died in 1984 aged only 34 years.

1990s

The last decade of the twentieth century saw a fall in the numbers of the congregation. The social life of the village was no longer centred around the church but, even so, the heritage that the church symbolised was appreciated. In 1990 two spotlights were installed and a community project was instigated by Lady Palmer and Jane Pattison, to encourage villagers to sponsor a hassock (a cushion to kneel on during prayers). All aspects of the work were executed by those in the village. Over five years, 192 hassocks were embroidered using twenty different designs; each hassock incorporated the name of those to whom it was dedicated. Revd Paul Broadbent, rector of the United Benefice of Gayton with Tiffield and Pattishall with Cold Higham from 1991, recognised that with an increase in the number of cremations, it would be desirable to have an area for interment, and ground was set aside in 1992 on the north side of the church. In 1994, a pedestal display cabinet with a Book of Remembrance was introduced to record the names of loved-ones in the churchyard. A new blue curtain was hung over the north door in 1995, replacing a procession of curtains dating back over the years; the first was in 1923 and had a red background and black fleur de lys design. In 1996, once more the roof was repaired and the church clock overhauled.

The next one thousand years!

The new Millennium was celebrated as a time to look back at the past and also forward to the future. It seemed fitting that the Tudor alabaster Tanfield tomb, with its lovely incised slab, was conserved for future generations to admire.

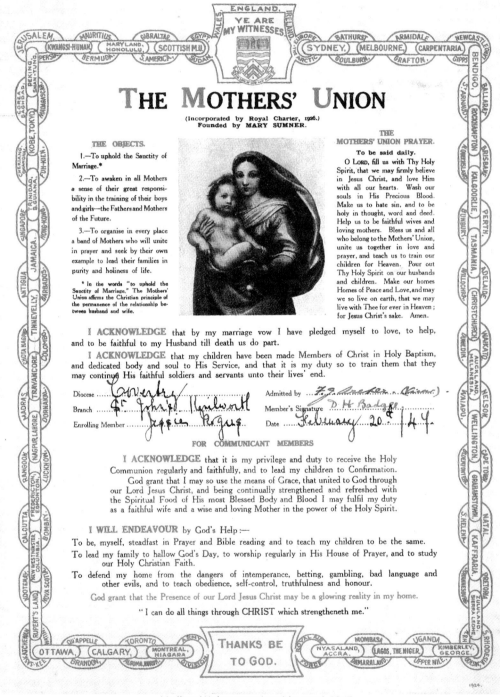

Mothers' Union membership card, 1947

Timeline for St Mary the Virgin, Gayton

1060	small west doorway of church tower has triangular shaped head (Royal Commission on the Historical Monuments of England RCHME)
1086	21 villagers with a priest (Domesday book p49)
1100	south wall of tower has single-light window with round head (RCHME)
early 13th century	font of Norman style (G Baker, *History of Northamptonshire* 1822)
Early English	piscina with trefoil head, stone shelf and ledge, with nail-head moulding (Baker)
Early English	south aisle added (RCHME)
Early English	small piscina with deeply chamfered head enclosing trefoil cusping (RCHME)
Early English	fine memorial slab with floriate cross (*Northampton Mercury* 1883)
early 14th century	full sized female figure of Scholastica de Gayton, under monumental arch (A Hartshorne, *Recumbent Monumental Effigies in Northamptonshire* 1876)
early 14th century	stone figure of a child, Mabila de Gayton (Baker)
mid 14th century	north wall of nave moved .5 metre to the south, and a north aisle added (RCHME)
mid 14th century	north chapel added as a chantry chapel (RCHME)
mid 14th century	oak effigy of Philip de Gayton (Baker)
1441	widow of lord of manor buried in the Blessed Virgin's cemetery (will, Trussell)
late 15th century	clerestory added (RCHME)
1510	rood screen (RM Sergeantson and HI Longden, *The Parish Churches and Religious Houses of Northamptonshire* 1913)
late 15th century	carved screen (Baker)
late 15th century	perpendicular sepulchred arch with marble slab monument of Robert Tanfield in south chancel (Sir Stephen Glynne, Church Notes)
1552	three bells of treble ring and one small saint bell in tower (Commissioners' Returns)
1570	church plate: silver cup and paten cover (Markham, *Church Plate*)
1583	alabaster monument with incised slab of Francis and Bridget Tanfield in chapel (Bridges)
1585	bell inscribed 'Give thanks to God always' (Bridges)
1594	bell inscribed 'Feare God and Obey the Lord' in Saxon capitals (Bridges)
1600	brass in the middle aisle of William Houghton, 17 December 1600 (Bridges)
1611	churchyard mounds with walls, pulpit, seating on north side, font cover and leading; printed matter (homilies, *Paraphase of Erasmus* and Statute for 5 November); references to chancel buttress and 'rain runs off churchyard under chancel door'; references to unpaved north chapel with rain coming in on tombs and seats unboarded (Church Survey)
1616	porch mentioned in legal document (Hawley 1/C/17)
1631	pulpit and reading seat described as 'not decent' (Church Survey)
1637	poor box or chest with three locks not available, and only one surplice (Church Survey Book)
1656	misericords from dissolved St James Abbey acquired (Visitation of Northamptonshire 1681)

1658	silver lidded flagon (WI Scrapbook)
1662	bell inscribed 'God Save King Charles' (Bridges)
17th century	Jacobean triple-decker pulpit (Faculty Plan)
17th century	nave roof has moulded tie beams and purlins (RCHME)
1708	church plate: silver salver or patten 18oz (Markham)
1720	chancel leaded and a porch on south, tiled; north chapel has at least two other monuments with no inscription; north chapel is Samwell's burial place, parted off from chancel and as big as the chancel (Bridges)
1725	faculty granted to raise height of steeple and hang six bells (Faculty vol 1 p241)
1726	bells inscribed 'William Ball Churchwarden 1726'; 'Prosperity to the Church of England 1726'; 'Peace and good neighbourhood 1726'; Glory be to God on high AR 1726'; 'the gift of the Reverend, Mr Gibbs Rector 1726'; 'In Dei laudem et Georgii regis honorem. Ex dono Thomœ Samwell Baronetti'
1726	Harlestone Stone £30 (churchwardens' accounts)
1744	faculty granted to erect a pew, upper end of north aisle (Faculty vol II p182)
1753	oval tablet on north wall of north chapel, Richard Kent of London (Baker)
1756	church whitewashed (churchwardens' accounts)
1759	Lockwood family memorial by Robert Blore (Baker)
1775	faculty for pew at east end, adjoining east wall and south wall in south aisle (Faculty vol III p132)
1780	oval tablet on north wall of north chapel, Richard Kent junior, died 8 January 1780 (Baker)
1801	small building extends from chancel/north chapel; shown as vestry on 1827 plan and demolished in 1828 (European Magazine)
1815	summary destruction of minstrels' gallery (H Davidson, Choirs, Bands and Organs 2003)
1816	removal of churchyard wall to incorporate an additional piece of land (churchwardens' accounts)
1817	deed and consecration for an additional burial ground contiguous with the old churchyard (Faculty V53-56)
1821	bell recast by voluntary subscription
1828	north chapel stated as being for many years in a state of extreme dilapidation; reconstructed nave and chancel roof; east window of north chapel and chancel reconstructed (Faculty V282)
1828	piscina with ogee trefoil head decorated with crockets and carried on miniature shafts, in the style of 14th century, in north chapel (RCHME)
1828	rector replaced the single door to the porch with folding doors; four old pews in the south aisle on the east side of the old porch to be re-fronted and floor raised; pulpit moved from north to south side of nave and no longer three decks; uniformly repewed and interior stone paved; Houghton brass moved to the north chapel; font moved from near old south porch to middle of entrance to the tower (churchwardens' accounts)
1828	new arch constructed between the north chapel and the chancel (Faculty V408)
1828	door and porch moved and reconstructed (churchwardens' accounts but Glynne states that the porch is of later date than the doorway)
c.1828	reredos carved in dark oak (Baker, although Pevsner disagrees)

1830 Fox Talbot donated Beauvais glass c.1643, and Flemish roundels c.1515, which are set in east window (Laycock Abbey 01959)

1836 chancel entered through lofty open arch from nave; north chapel now communicates with both north aisle and chancel; east end of the north chapel is converted into a vestry and separated by a carved medieval screen (Baker)

1849 clock donated and fixed high up on tower (Whellan's *Directory* 1849)

1862 lower part of the tower opens to the nave by 'rude and small' pointed arch; east window of south aisle is a circle with flowing tracery; between north chapel and the north aisle of the nave is a 'Tudor-shaped' arch (Glynne)

1866 decorated buttress over door in north wall of nave incorporates a dedication stone; in north wall of nave are traces of a circular headed door, long since walled up (*Northampton Mercury* 12 May 1866)

1871 new organ (Whellan's *Directory* 1874)

1881 faculty to remove plaster ceilings; remove gallery floors and surface levels with new steps, tiles and heating flues; for a new heating chamber; to add seats, refix font and pulpit, and build structural stone shelf in east wall of chancel; to add new upper stage to tower and stairs to tower; for a vestry and organ chamber; to construct arches in east wall of south aisle and in south wall of chancel (Faculty ML1119 p510)

1881 chancel roof rebuilt following line of early roof; rood screen preserved in vestry(RCHME)

1881 east window of south aisle removed when the vestry was built

1882 three largest bells rehung by John Taylor & Co., with new fittings and frame reconstructed using old timber

1883 second stage of tower has two light windows with blind trefoils over; belfry (RCHME)

1883 discovery of door to rood loft in south wall of the nave, and of a piscina in the south aisle; removal of west gallery and tower arch opened out; Flemish glass installed in windows of the north chapel; east window in chancel and the lancet window in the tower remained to be glazed (*Northampton Mercury* 3 February 1883)

1885 buttresses to east wall of chancel stated as being nineteenth century (RCHME)

1889 a memorial window to Richard Eykyn installed in chancel; west end small window erected by Thomas Eykyn (Kelly's *Directory* 1894)

1908 liquid cement forced between the stonework of the tower (*Northampton Echo*)

1908 bell frame reconstructed by John Taylor & Co., who reused much of the old timber

1910 tower alterations and clock lowered. Tower is crowned by a battlement parapet with elaborate angle pinnacles and gargoyles (RCHME and oral history)

1920 faculty to erect First World War memorial tablet

1921 silver spoon donated by Arthur Eykyn (WI *Scrapbook*)

1929 faculty to install electric light in the church

1930	bell frame and fittings found to be defective with grub and beetle resulting in 'bad going order of peal' (John Taylor & Co)
1930	bells rehung (WI *Scrapbook*)
1931	bells recast: 'WF Stokes MA Rector, JM Major Lucas, WA Ratledge, churchwardens'
1935	curtains removed from baptistry (*Deanery Magazine* October 1955)
1936	faculty to install McClary Pipeless Heating in an underground extension of the crypt
1952	burial in new portion of graveyard, 27 August (*Deanery Magazine* October)
1953	silver chalice and paten dated 1569, presented by Roger and Mary Eykyn; silver chalice and paten dated 1901-02 (WI *Scrapbook*)
1953	children's corner with pictures and books (*Deanery Magazine* March)
1954	organ appeal. Starmer Shaw & Son win contract (*Deanery Magazine* July)
1954	organ dedicated. Description of procession with a peal of bells and flag flying in the tower (*Deanery Magazine* October)
1954	boiler, flue and grid overhauled in April; candlesticks gifted in August (*Deanery Magazine*)
1955	oak table made to hold the alms box; service books, altar coverings and curtains etc., presented for the north chapel; brackets made on the end of chancel stalls for processional cross and banner; baptistry curtains dedicated at Patronal Festival; brass tablet of William Houghton, 1660 replated (*Deanery Magazine*, various months)
1967	faculty to renew wood block flooring and timber bearers under the pews; place a wooden altar table, which had been gifted, in north chapel; instal an aumbry in wall of sanctuary
1973	fund started to electrify clock winding system and treat timbers in church and belfry (*Village Circular*, August)
1984	faculty for oak screen in the arch leading from the nave to the west end of the tower; jambs of former south doorway found below west window of the south aisle; font sited at west end of south aisle of the nave (RCHME)
1994	faculty for a pedestal display cabinet to display the Book of Remembrance
1996	faculty to overhaul church clock
1996	faculty to repair roof
2000	faculty to conserve the Tanfield tomb
2005	*Further Glimpses of Gayton, a Northamptonshire Church and Community* written by Rita Poxon and launched at Churchale, 8 September

Notes and references

Chapter one: Setting the scene

1   John Morris (editor), *Domesday Book, Northamptonshire* (1979), p228a
2   N(orthamptonshire) R(ecord) O(ffice), Churchwardens' Accounts and Vestry Minutes, ZA8330
3   JC Cox and CB Ford, *The Parish Churches of England* (1947), p39
4   R and N Muir, *Hedgerows* (1987), pp48-50
5   N Pevsner *Northamptonshire* (1961), pp212-14
6   P Ziegler, *The Black Death* (1968), pp174-75
7   A Hartshorne *Recumbent Monumental Effigies in Northamptonshire* (1876), pp51-52
8   Northampton and Oakham Architectural Society, *Sanctuary Seekers in Northamptonshire* (c.1913), p220

Chapter two: The uncertain horror of death

9   The National Archives, PROB 11-42A 102-99 and 100 Welles 12 December 1558
10 RM Sergeantson and HI Longden, *The Parish Churches and Religious Houses of Northamptonshire* (1913), pp 109-10. St Nicholas was the patron saint of children and his feast day was celebrated on 6 December
11 E Duffy, *The Stripping of the Altars* (1992), p407

Chapter three: Confusion and change

12 NRO, George Clarke Sketches c.1930
13 *Northampton Mercury* 12 May 1866, p7 c3-4

Chapter four: Ding, dong, bell!

14 DS Sutherland, *Northamptonshire Stone* (2003), p53

Chapter five: Parish work

15 L(incolnshire) R(ecord) O(ffice), Hawley 6/2 1757
16 L Munby, *How Much is that Worth?* (1996), p38; FF Waddy, *A History of Northampton General Hospital 1743-1948* (1974)
17 JH Bettey, *Church and Parish* (1987), p98
18 K Thomas, *Magic and Religion* (1991), p318
19 F Anthonie, *Apologie* (1616), p36
20 J Cotta, *Cotta contra Anthonium* (1623), p59
21 NRO, Gayton Parish Register, 132p/4
22 *ibid*
23 J Bridges, *The History of Northamptonshire* (1791), p262
24 WE Tate, *The Parish Chest* (1983 edition), p172
25 NRO, Vestry Minute Book 1827-1956, 132p/167
26 NRO, Northampton Wills First Series Book W fo 65 MW16, Gregory Warren 1590
27 NRO, Gayton Parish Register, 132p/4
28 Tate, *The Parish Chest*, p106
29 NRO, Butler Family Papers, ZA 8549 p2
30 NRO, PCC Minute Book 1921-1955, 132p/160

Chapter six: War and peace

31 AG Matthews, *Walker Revised* (1848), p277
32 Towcester and District Local History Society, *Towcester: The Story of an English Country Town* (1995), p125
33 *Oxford Dictionary of National Biography* (internet 2005), Sir John Lambe
34 AG Matthews, *Calamy Revised* (1934 edition), p89
35 *Oxford Dictionary of National Biography* (internet 2005), Samuel Clarke
36 H Barber, *A Forgotten Chapter in English Church History* (1898), p17

Chapter seven: Colour and glitter

37   R Marks, *The Medieval Stained Glass of Northamptonshire* (1998), p 77
38   Laycock, Fox Talbot Museum; Laycock Abbey Collection, LA41-022, Correspondence of William Henry Fox Talbot, 25 March 1841, Doc no: 04226
39   Fox Talbot Museum, Laycock Abbey Collection, LA41-022, Correspondence of William Henry Fox Talbot, 25 March 1841, Doc no: 01761
40   W Cole, *A Catalogue of Netherlandish and N European Roundels in Britain* (1993), pp86-88 ; Fox Talbot Museum, Laycock Abbey Collection LA41-022, Correspondence of William Henry Fox Talbot, 25 March 1841, Doc no: 01959
41   G Baker, *History of Northamptonshire*, Vol 4 (1822), p280
42   NRO, Butler Family Papers, ZA 8549
43   Rita Poxon Collection, Kennard Letters, 20 Sept 1841
44   *Wetton's Guide to Northampton and its Vicinity* (1849), p167
45   William Whellan and Co., *History, Gazetteer and Directory of Northamptonshire* (1849), p549
46   Victoria and Albert Museum Archives, AAD/1977/1/47
47   Gayton Women's Institute, *Scrapbook*, 1953

Chapter eight: Maintenance work

48   LRO, Hawley 6/2 1757
49   NRO, Churchwardens' Accounts and Vestry Minutes 1726-1829, ZA 8830
50   NRO, Church Survey Book Brackley Deanery, Box 622 Vol 2
51   *Northampton Herald*, 27 July 1906
52   A Mee, *The King's England: Northamptonshire* (1945), p129

Chapter nine: Music, music, music

53   E Duffy, *The Stripping of the Altars* (1992), p369
54   NRO, Vestry Minute Book 1827-1956, 132p/167
55   NRO, Churchwardens' Accounts and Vestry Minutes, ZA8330
56   NRO, Butler Family Papers, ZA 8548
57   H Davidson, *Choirs, Bands and Organs* (2003)
58   Eric White Collection, *Brackley Deanery Magazine* February 1954
59   *Northampton Mercury*, 3 February 1883, p8 col 1-2
60   Eric White Collection, *Brackley Deanery Magazine*, 1906-1920

Chapter ten: Victorian solutions

61   *Northampton Herald*, 31 July 1875
62   NRO, PCC Minute Book 1921-1955, 132p/160
63   NRO, Sir Stephen Glynne's unpublished Church Notes, ZB 376/2 Vol 42/75; *Brackley Deanery Magazine* April 1938
64   *Northampton Mercury*, 12 May 1866, p7 c3-4
65   NRO, Butler Family Papers, ZA 8549 p2
66   NRO, Abstract of Education Returns, 1818, 1833
67   *Gayton Church*, booklet (1958)
68   Wiltshire and Swindon Record Office, Haden & Co, Order Book, 29 Jun 1882, ref 1325/41
69   NRO, Churchwardens' Minute Book, 6 April 1921-8 May 1928, 132p/162

Chapter eleven: Twentieth century concerns

70   *Gayton Church*, booklet (1958)
71   NRO, Peterborough Diocese, C14 Orders in Council, 361, 388
72   NRO, Faculty, *Modern Gayton*

Illustrations

Front cover: The Parish Church of St Mary the Virgin, Gayton, from the south-east. Photograph by Rod Poxon
Church inventory 1552, by kind permission of the National Archives, E117/7/2/3

Back cover: Villagers who are closely connected with activities in support of the church, 2005. Photographs by Rod Poxon

Top left: Sam Hartley, Steven Huckle, Breeshey and Viv Hartley, Pippa Taylor, Elaine Huckle, Catherine and Andy Hartley

Top right: Peter James, Tony Barrett, John Allen and Eric White

Bottom left: John Shaw, Martin Church, Jonathon Taylor and Joan McCarthy

Bottom right: Joan Jeffery, Penny Taylor and Anna Fox

All photographs are by Rod Poxon, LRPS, except:

Margaret Ratledge Collection, p1

Rita Poxon Collection, pp20, 45, 53, 74

Rita Poxon Collection, gift of Mary Morris, pp46, 68

The incumbent and Parochial Church Council of Gayton for permission to use documents held at the Northamptonshire Record Office (NRO): (ZA8830) p29; (132p/179) p35; (ZA8827) p37

The Diocese of Peterborough for permission to use documents held at the NRO: (Gayton Faculties, vol v-282) pp56-57

Wendy Briglin Collection, pp59, 64

Index

Eleanor cross, 8
Electricity, 34, 62, 67, 70
Elizabeth I, 14-17
Elizabeth II, 24
Embroidery and Sewing Guild, 70
Enclosure, 30, 32
Enville, 42
Eramus, 25
Evacuee, 52
Evans, Glyn, 73
Evans, Mr, 54
Eyden, Mr W, 69
Eykyn family, 44, 46
Eykyn, Arthur, 46-67
Eykyn, Mary, 44, 46
Eykyn, Richard, 44, 62
Eykyn, Roger, 44, 46, 60-62, 71
Eykyn, Susanna, 44, 62
Eykyn, Thomas, 44, 61

Facer, Thomas, 23, 50, 62
Faculty, 23
Farmer, 6, 26, 34
Faulkener, Duncan, 54
Fiennes, Ingelram de, 6
Finials, 70
Finton, Widow, 32
Fisher, Mrs, 52
Fishmonger, 25
Fitzhugh, Richard, 50
Fitzmaurice, Henry Petty, 43
Fiveways, 60, 69
Flag, 54
Flagon, 45-46
Floor, 7, 47, 62, 70-71
Folwell, Mrs, 64
Folwell, 'Pem', 55
Font, 3-4, 18-19, 40-41, 58, 62, 70
Forman, Thomas, 31
Foster, Joan, 12-13, 51
Foster, William, 13
Fosters Booth, 23, 66
Fowkes, Martin, 32
Fox Talbot, William Henry, 43
Fox, 34
Foxe, 25
France, 44, 67

Gable, Julia Helen, 71
Gardener, Francis, 31
Gardner, Revd Thomas, 51
Gardner, Thomas, 50
Gates, 47
Gayton de, 8
Gayton House, 26, 38, 44, 46, 58
Gayton National School, 61
Gayton Rectory, 44
Gayton, Henry de, 1-2
Gayton, Mabila de, 7
Gayton, Philip de, 6, 8, 11-12, 43, 59

Gayton, Scholastica de, 8
Gayton, Thomas de, 7
Gayton, William de, 6
George II, 24
George, Benjamin, 50
George, Joseph, 36, 50
George, Mr, 34
George, Mrs, 64
George, Samuel, 50
George, Walter, 50
George, William, 36, 50, 61
Gibbs, Ben, 47-48
Gibbs, Revd William junior, 21, 23, 26, 28
Gibbs, Revd William senior, 26, 28, 47
Gifford, Amy, 40
Gifford, Ann, 39
Gifford, Revd Richard, 26, 39, 40-41
Gifford, Roger, 40
Gilbert and Sullivan, 72
Glazier, 47, 71
Gloucester, 23
Gloucestershire, 22
Glynne, Sir Stephen, 58
Goff, Mr L, 73
Gold, 26
Goodyer, Miss, 72
Goodyer, Mr, 72
Goodyer, Mrs, 72
Goosey, Mr, 49
Gordon, Nicholas, 71
Gramophone, 54
Grand National, 72
Gravestone, 28, 50
Green, John, 35
Green, Mrs, 64, 72
Green, Thomas, 32
Green, Trevor, 71
Green, William, 30
Greens Norton, 48
Griffith, Anna Maria, 25
Griffith, Mr, 34
Griffith, Pheasant, 50
Griffith, Revd Walter, 25
Griffith, William, 36, 48, 50
Gudgeon, Cornelius, 50
Guisne, de, 6
Gunn, Spencer, 72

Haden & Co, 62
Haig, Earl, 69
Haldenby, John de, 25
Hall, Mrs, 64
Hammell, Mrs, 64
Hancock, Mrs, 64
Hand bells, 51
Harlestone stone, 23, 48
Harlestone, 23, 48
Harpole, 31
Harris, John, 50
Harris, William, 36